Trusting to Luck

This is the story of how I grew up in Cambridge and spent my gap year achieving my romantic dream of getting a job in Paris and hitch-hiking to Greece. Many things could – and did – go wrong on my journey. And, as the account of my childhood will show, I possessed none of the qualities that would recommend me to undertake this adventure, beyond confidence, luck, and the support of tolerant parents.

In April 1961, a month after my nineteenth birthday, I got a job selling the international edition of the New York Times outside the Musee du Louvres in Paris, a job which led to the most exciting adventure of my life. But before I tell you about the job, I want to tell you about some of the ingredients poured into the soup of my teenage mind by my upbringing, and the spirit of the sixties, that made such a job seem like the fulfilment of a romantic dream.

To begin at the beginning. I imagine birth as an event like the big bang which scatters your genes into the future, where events harden them into the separate facets of your character. These facets form the upward spiral of your life – moulded by your actions and circumstances, but still determining the way you react and behave. Life is a voyage towards self-recognition.

My early life – or that part of it which I remember - was shaped by my parents who, one year after the war, when I was three years old, moved to 74 Huntingdon Road, Cambridge – 'seventy-four with the pea-green door'- as my mother kept reminding us. My father already had a job as a physics teacher at the Leys Public school at the other end of town – though he moved with my mother to Inverness during the war to become a radar officer in the Royal Navy. My parents were a well-liked and handsome couple — as I was so often told by their friends — but their attitude to life, as I later discovered, had been partly shaped by adversity. My father was the second of three boys whose father had died in the final year of the First World War. Because he turned out to be the clever one, his family made sacrifices to enable him to win a scholarship to study physics at Downing College, Cambridge. His elder brother, Jack, lent him the money to help him pay the deposit on the house in Huntingdon Road.

My mother too had a difficult childhood, for reasons I only discovered much later in life. Like my father, she was the clever one in her family, who won a scholarship to study mathematics at Girton College, Cambridge. We never saw her elder brother, Charles, who sent us regular presents on birthdays or at Christmas, or her younger sister, Vera, who married a bus driver. It felt as if my mother wanted to keep her family out of the picture because she was ashamed of them. During her childhood, her family moved around a lot because her father never settled in one place. Her mother took temping jobs as a secretary and earned some sympathy from her children for struggling to bring up her family unaided. My mother only discovered in her first year at university that the reason she seldom saw her father was that her mother wasn't his wife but his mistress. This was a matter of great shame in the 1930s and disrupted the relationship between their two families. And it caused a lingering irritation every time my parents felt obliged to invite my grandmother to stay, which she did for three or four months a year, occupying the tiny bedroom at the back of the house, beyond my own, which my father also used as his study.

My grandmother was a sprightly woman in her early seventies, as I remember her when she first came to live with us. She retained certain habits from the late Victorian era, like scrambling out of bed to stand up when she heard the national anthem played on the radio, or declining a second helping with the words 'No thank-you, I've had an ample sufficiency.' Her face was powdered and pink with rouge, which made my mother seethe with irritation, but she was still a game old lady who was once caught climbing the apple tree. And I taught her to say 'I've chased a bug around a tree. I'll get his blood. He knows I will,' as fast as she could, and – at the third attempt - she found it deliciously naughty.

The fact that both my parents were brought up by single mothers shaped their parental ambitions. They were going to do things properly! As far as I was concerned, this meant in my father's eyes that I was going to be a real boy and a good citizen, and in my mother's eyes, I was destined for Oxford or Cambridge. I think her fixed idea of my abilities was based on the fact that when I was two years old and a doctor came to our house to lance my boil, I was able to say in a posh voice "It's all right, Dr Mason. I'm feeling quite better now."

My mother's first child was a girl. In fact, she had been expecting twins, but the boy died and Ann was the one to survive. I remember my mother, years later, saying regretfully how Ann had asked her after I was born, "Aren't you going to cuddle me anymore?" And then, of course, she did. But it never occurred to me until many years later that my mother treated Ann unfairly – in fact, Ann and I very often quarrelled. But in hindsight, I wonder if there was something irrational about my mother's disapproval of Ann, as if she'd have preferred the surviving twin to be a boy. She changed her attitude later in life when she came to recognise Ann's solid qualities that the rest of us failed to possess.

I don't remember much of my early years – just memories of memories. I remember being hospitalised at the age of two because I got a toy trumpet stuck in my throat. My parents were pleased after the event because it meant that I jumped the queue to have my tonsils and adenoids removed. All I can remember is sitting at the bottom of the stairs knowing that something had gone wrong and then lying in a hospital bed being greeted by a young nurse who offered me a sweet, and then betrayed me by sticking a needle in my arm. We all spent some of our earlier years being confined to bed with German measles and whooping cough, measles and mumps, but we didn't get any of the allergies suffered by later generations whose standards of cleanliness may have weakened their resistance to germs.

I tested this theory to its limits five years later on our annual camping holiday in Norfolk, when I gathered the loose straw that covered the field beyond our tent and used branches and straw to create a network of tunnels, opening into hidden chambers where I spent a good part of each day dreaming of adventures. Several weeks later, in Cambridge, standing beside the bus stop with my grandmother on return from a visit to the Botanical Gardens, I had a strange sensation of being separated from the people all around me behind an invisible wall. I could see them, but I wasn't part of them. By the time I got home, I began to shiver and become feverish, and a doctor was called round to stick a needle, pumped full of penicillin in my bottom, and I was consigned to several weeks in bed. I had Urticaria, apparently, which has surely given me a lifetime's immunity to dirt.

At the age of four, I fell in love with Elizabeth Taylor – not the famous actress, but a girl in my kindergarten class. I think the experience lasted about an hour; a long time at that age. I was mortified when I heard Ann gleefully reporting the news to my parents. I also remember the snow which fell heavily that year. We all walked up the Huntingdon road away from town and joined a large group of families using sledges and tea trays to slide down the slopes of the University Farm. Then a wild boar was spotted heading in our direction and we scattered amid shouts and shrieks of alarm. Later that winter, my father stopped on the way back from Church and crossed the road to pick up two German prisoners of war who spent Christmas with us while waiting to be repatriated. They gave me a wooden cart as a Christmas present, which they had painted in red and yellow.

When I was five years old, my father bought me a clockwork train set for Christmas. He went to church that morning – not because he was a committed Christian, but because he thought it was the right thing to do. Despite his obvious intelligence, my father deferred to others on many opinions about life and how one ought to behave. I sat alone at the dining room table, unwrapping my present and taking the train and the carriages out of the box. My mother must have been around somewhere, probably attending to my three-year-old sister, Sarah, on the other side of the folding screen that divided the sitting room from the dining-room. My eight-year-old sister Ann was probably at home too – unless she had gone with my father to church.

I can only remember sitting at the table dismantling my train set. I started with the train itself, pulling off the wheels and placing them in a neat pile. I did the same with the carriages, adding the wheels to the pile. Then I noticed that the train and each of its carriages could be pulled apart too. I levered the train off its metal base and did the same with the carriages. There must have been other elements – if so, I'm sure I managed to find them. I succeeded in making several orderly piles of wheels and bases and coach parts and so on. I don't know how long it took me to demolish my first train set.

I don't remember if I felt guilty about what I'd done. I think the guilt came afterwards when I saw the disgust and shock on my father's face. He had bought me my first 'boy's present' and I had ruined it. That didn't stop him making me a butterfly cage with a wooden frame and a perforated metal frontage with the holes small enough to prevent the caterpillars escaping. I gathered these caterpillars from the stinging nettles that grew in a small plot of waste ground behind our back garden. I stuffed them in the cage and left them to feed on a pile of nettles until, one by one, they crawled up the sides of the cage and turned into chrysalises hanging like tiny paper lanterns from the top of the cage. Then, one summer afternoon, the first tortoiseshell butterfly broke free of its chrysalis, and I opened the cage and sat and watched in wonder as it floated up and away over the garden fence. Then another butterfly broke free, and another and another. By some mysterious process, they all hatched at more or less the same time. There must have been at least fifty of them, gathered in a swarm of red, black and white, floating up and away over the garden fence.

My father, being a physics teacher, was also able to use the materials from his science lab to make me a transistor radio with earphones so that I was able to lie in bed at night listening to 'The Archers' or a scary story about voyagers in space which gave me nightmares. Another gift from this practical man, who constantly harped on about his shortcomings, was the art of gardening. Ann and I were both given small sections of flower bed to look after, and pocket money to buy seeds. I don't remember what seeds I chose for myself, but I do remember planting mustard seeds in Ann's garden so that they grew and grew, and dwarfed her tiny seedlings. I think she'd lost her interest in gardening by this stage, so my treachery went unnoticed.

On a more practical note, my father did all the cooking. He made good use of what was available in the early fifties, making 'toad in a hole', cod in a Bechamel sauce, bacon, eggs and sausages, with desserts such as Flummery, pancakes and apple pie and scones and mince pies and the like. The milkman would stop in a horse-drawn carriage outside our front door and deliver bread, milk and small bottles of fresh orange juice – recommended by the socialist minister of health.

Sometimes the milk was sour but my father just told us to drink it and not be 'faddy.' My mother refused to go near the kitchen until the walls were scrubbed down and repainted. Several years later, when this task was achieved, she would disappear after a meal, varying her excuses from a headache to a sore finger, or simply wandering upstairs.

Pleasing my father was something that occupied my thoughts off and on up to the age of 13 or 14. I say 'off and on' because I often annoyed him intensely in ways which he was very quick to point out and I don't think it worried me that much. He kept saying "stop showing off" or 'take that 'aren't- I- clever look' off your face." I think that part of the problem was that my mother wanted me to be clever, while my father wanted me to be a normal small boy who just did what he was told. My mother did her best to push me ahead by reading me all sorts of children's books and even making a coloured chart of multiplication tables right up to twelve times twelve so that I won temporary fame by winning the tables competition ahead of the older age groups in our kindergarten.

My father was a popular teacher at the Leys. But, although outwardly at ease among his colleagues, he always complained of feeling inadequate. Other people always had more to offer in terms of talents or achievements and were above all more confident than himself. My mother kept calling him 'Uriah Heep' because he was so annoyingly humble. He admired and resented my confidence, which was certainly more obvious to him than it was to me. Perhaps what annoyed him most was that I was always 'getting away with it', teasing or making silly mistakes and not getting punished for them. This annoyance reached its peak when my grandmother came to stay. What annoyed my father most was that my grandmother singled me out from birth as her favourite and had no time for my elder sister, who treated her with more respect than I did. She was always taking me aside and giving me sweets or small sums of money and, on one occasion, she was even discovered 'making my bed.' When my father heard the news, he went red in the face and rushed up the stairs to unmake it, which left me feeling bitter and disgusted.

My father's attitude towards me was ambivalent. My elder sister thought he was envious of me because of my supposed confidence and because my mother often stuck up for me, but I think this was only half the story. He wanted me to conform to his image of 'a real boy' – the way boys used to be when he grew up in the country with his two brothers and his widowed mother. He wanted me to be good with my hands, go fishing, climb trees, ride a bicycle, throw snowballs without needing to wear gloves, and be a role model for my younger brother and sister who were just too young to need to conform to any model at all.

He ran along beside me when he bought me my first bicycle at the age of six, but he did admit to being pleased, shortly afterwards, when someone walked in through the back gate and stole it. It had cost him ten pounds – half a working man's wage at that time - and he could reclaim the money off insurance. When the bike mysteriously reappeared, I think I was more pleased than he was, because he realised that he could have bought a secondhand bike for a quarter of the price.

I was in my third year at kindergarten by this time, which was just 400 yards away, on the opposite side of the road leading towards the town. Byron House was one of three substantial villas owned by the descendants of Charles Darwin, each surrounded by woods and lined with elm trees facing onto the road. From my parents' bedroom window, you could hear the mournful caw of the rooks as they flew to and from their nests high up in the trees.

One of the classmates I remember as well as Elizabeth Taylor, was an impish little girl with short black hair called Monika Dirac, the daughter of the Nobel prizewinning scientist who discovered quantum theory. Her father conformed to the public image of a boffin; the postman once mistook him for the gardener because he was sitting in the apple tree when he called round. He was a simple man, utterly without pride or sense of importance, who once drove round to our house and gave my mother a second-hand fridge at a time when Monica was one of her pupils at the County High School for Girls. I met Monica and Elizabeth years later when they were students.

The headmistress of Byron House gave the children and their parents the entertaining challenge, over the course of the Easter holidays, of finding as many different specimens as they could out of a list of about 75 wild flowers, so I needed my bike for that. The quest sent us all over Cambridgeshire and my parents were as consumed by the challenge as we were.

The most exciting moment came as we approached the end of our search and we had to go further a field to hunt for the last, elusive flowers on our list. My sister Ann had a book of wild flowers and her interest in flowers persisted longer than mine.

At the age of seven, I went to St Faiths, the Prep school that prepared boys for the Leys. As the two schools were connected, my father was entitled to a fifty per cent reduction in fees. Money was tight for a lot of parents in the fifties, so many of them – like my parents – attended the annual school jumble sale - to buy our caps, our striped red and black jackets, and our sports shirts second hand. St Faiths was one degree posher than the Leys as some of the boys – mainly the sons of academics - went on to more distinguished public schools like Eton, Marlborough or Winchester.

I took the bus 106 to my new school from a few yards down from our house. I was always in love with someone, and for a short time I fell in love with the young bus conductress. She had long black hair, and she always chatted with me as she dropped me off on the final leg of my journey - what seemed like a long walk to school. Since I have never had a good sense of direction, for the return journey, I waited on the wrong side of the road one day and found myself heading miles in the opposite direction from home. The conductress was very kind and made sure that I stayed close to her until the bus completed its journey and I got off at the right stop opposite our house.

My first teachers at St Faith's included Monsieur Madge, the French teacher with a comfortably rounded stomach, who sat back in his chair and extended a ruler between his stomach and the desk. He sometimes lined us up against the wall and asked the boy at the head of the line a question in French. If the answer was acceptable, the boy got to sit down. If not, he went to the back of the line. Another teacher, who shall be nameless, taught us scripture. He started from the first book of Genesis, cruised through Exodus and shortly afterwards made his own exodus after being caught in flagrante delicto exposing himself to one of the boarders in my class. I saw him many years later, supervising a football match at a rival prep school. Pastures new, I thought! Although homosexuality, even among adults, was a crime in those days, schools simply passed the bad apples down the food chain. Our English teacher, Mr Warburton, briefly went off piste to rave about his religious beliefs, but they merely seemed to affect his sanity. He spoke, like a man inspired, about the wonders of his faith, and then, one day, for no apparent reason, lined us up against the wall of the gym and beat each of us with a ruler. Well, there may have been a reason, but I don't think any of us stopped to consider it. It was actually my ruler and a rather a long one at that! It attracted his attention the moment I brought it to school and, whenever I made a cheeky remark, he would crook a finger in my direction and ask me to stand up and give it to him so that he could use it on my hand.

Then there was poor Mr Fletcher, a conscientious but hesitant teacher, who kept looking up from his desk and saying 'Stop that!' with a look in his eyes that suggested he hadn't much hope of achieving his objective. Mr Fletcher, who taught us maths, was known as 'Fishy Fletcher.' Tom Griffiths, the boy sitting next to me, once got up and started walking out five minutes before the end of the lesson. "What are you doing?" asked Mr Fletcher. "The lesson's not over yet!" Griffiths stopped at the door with an air of mild surprise and said, "Sorry, Sir. Just fishful winking." Mr Fletcher gave a patient smile, as the class erupted in laughter, and just waited for him to return to his desk.

Mike Bayon taught us Latin and Greek. He was an inspiring teacher, both in the classroom and on the sports field. He was a handsome man with classical features and the fire of enthusiasm in his eyes – which could switch in an instant to a smouldering rage. He had been a navigator on bomber planes during the war, and the quality he most admired was courage. I am afraid my courage is more on a par with bold Sir Brian's in 'King Arthur and The Knights of the Holy Grail' who 'when danger raised his ugly head, bravely turned his tail and fled.' Fortunately, when Mike Bayon was around, I managed to keep this deficiency under the radar.

On one occasion, when watching small boys performing on the rugby field, Mike Bayon spotted a large boy, that he regarded as spoilt and useless, backing out of the scrum and complaining of a pain in his leg. His reaction was immediate and violent. He grabbed the boy by the shoulders, shook him until he fell to the ground, then picked him up and, in a volley of precisely chosen words, proceeded to demolish his character, until the boy stood with his head down, looking shaken and cowed. "There's nothing wrong with your leg!"

Mike Bayon declared. There he was mistaken, as the hospital later confirmed.

In the classroom, despite his sporadic rages, Mike Bayon was a brilliant teacher, someone who was able to convey the knowledge of a university professor in a way that was amusing or exciting to boys aged from eight to twelve. He taught us about the geography of Greece and Rome, and the battles and myths, and he got us translating Virgil and Livy, Herodotus and Euripides. I wonder how many other children have had their paths through life determined by one or two inspiring teachers. On one occasion, Mike Bayon switched to teaching us English, and he asked us to write a story. I became thoroughly engrossed in my homework on this rare occasion and went on writing some extended piece of juvenile drivel until my father interrupted me and said, "Look, you've got to finish the thing now! Just write 'They motored on into the story.'"

I meekly followed his advice and on the next day, or the day after, Mike Bayon read the story aloud to the class. He was so impressed that I glowed with praise until he asked, "Did anyone help you with this?" Imbued with prep school honour, I had to admit, "My father helped me a bit." He nodded in an understanding way, and said, "Well, I liked it all except for the last sentence - 'They motored on into the story.'" I felt done on all fronts. However, I was better pleased by his final sentence on my school report that year: 'his brilliance shines through the cloak of his laziness.'

Well, that's what you pay for when you send your children to private schools – that confidence boosting shot of adrenalin that helps you shine at interviews. My father didn't have to make a joke of it for me to know that it wasn't true. I was surrounded by boys cleverer than myself and I wasn't actually lazy. It was just that my intelligence went on and off like a flickering light; shining for a brief moment, then spluttering and fading away. It was not long before my younger brother was able to beat me at any game which demanded intelligence, for my mind still goes blank at some point where abstract reasoning is involved. But there was that occasional flash of light when I knew I had said or written something more insightful.

Mike Bayon came to my aid one day, shortly after the sweet shops reopened, and I brought an enormous paper bag full of aniseed balls to school. In the middle of the lesson, the bag burst and the aniseed balls bounced on the floor beneath my desk and scattered across the room. Chaos erupted as small boys dropped on their hands and knees, gathering as many of these small objects as they could find and stuffing them into their mouths. Mike Bayon was furious but – to my intense relief – his anger was not directed at me, but at my classmates. What they were doing amounted to stealing!

The teacher whose classes I most dreaded was Mr Gibbons, a martinet with a high squeaky voice who taught us geography. Our homework mainly involved drawing blue lines around islands and continents to indicate the sea. As all our work involved staring at an atlas of the world with the British Isles on the left and America on the right, it wasn't until I was 29 years old and heading for a teaching post in New York that I realised that we wouldn't be heading east over California but west over Ireland to reach our destination. I suspect that many of us may have similar, extraordinary gaps in our knowledge.

When I was eight years old, we went on our first camping holiday in Norfolk. This involved placing all our equipment in a taxi – cases, an old army ridge tent and a small white toilet tent – and cycling to join the taxi at the station. My parents took the two younger children on their bicycles. The bicycles and baggage had to be loaded onto the train at Cambridge station, then onto another train at Norwich, which took us to North Walsham.

From there we unloaded our baggage into a taxi and cycled to our final destination, a small field in the village of Knapton. The field belonged to Farmer May and on our first year it was sown with sugar beet. We set up camp on the edge of the field, with the lane on our left and the church on the other side of the lane. To the immediate right of our tent was a wooden hut on wheels where my father sat and swore as he struggled to cook our breakfast on a primus stove in the early hours of the morning. At the far edge of the field to our right was a sheltered barn where we could hear the steady drone of the seven farm labourers early in the morning planning their day in their Norfolk accents. And at the other end of the field, in the corner overlooking the lane, was a sturdy oak tree to which I developed a Wordsworthian attachment, climbing the eight feet or so to the point where the thick branches spread, offering a comfortable space to sit and daydream.

Directly behind our tent, in one of the cottages belonging to the farm, lived the foreman, Mr Stewart, with his wife and four children of a similar age to ourselves. Ann quickly made a friend of the eldest, Janet, and I played a lot with Ruth, her skinny sister, the same age as myself, who ran around in a skimpy dress followed by her younger brother, Eric. Janet and Ruth were both heading for the local grammar school in North Walsham. Ruth was a bit of a scold. She constantly reproached Eric for any form of mischief, warning him in a shrill voice, "You'll get wronged if you do that." Getting wronged meant getting a belting from her dad's strap. They had a friend called Bruce, the son of another farm labourer, who joined us in some of our games. He had a round, unwashed face and a permanent shifty grin, which he may have got from regular beatings from his father.

Camping in Knapton gave me a brief glimpse into another world. For five weeks and two days we played games outside in the fields or cycled two miles along lanes, edged with high, grassy banks strewn with wild flowers, to the seaside in Mundesley. My father woke me up once at four in the morning so that we could cycle off and hunt for mushrooms to fry with the rest of our breakfast. Hunting among the fields, damp with dew in the misty morning air, was one of the most exciting events of my childhood.

And then, at the end of our stay, came the thrill of returning home and finding our small garden, with its ageing pear tree in the centre and its three apple trees tucked in behind, laden with fruit. I can still remember my moment of anguish the following year, as my mother stood beside the chest of drawers on the landing, packing clothes into cases, when she suddenly said with a bright smile, "Yes, we'll be going to Knapton tomorrow." I wanted to know for how long and, when I worked out it would be for four weeks and six days., I felt gutted. She had snatched three days from our holiday!

My mother was very protective of us in some ways. When my Aunt Mabel died, I didn't hear about it straight away. Our parents presumably attended the funeral in our absence. I can also remember a sweet girl of eleven or twelve once coming to our house, never to return. My mother said sorrowfully that she had eaten a poisoned toadstool and was being treated in hospital. My sister told me years later that she had died of cancer. Perhaps because of this protection, it only really struck home to me when I was eight or nine years old that death was something we all had to face in the end. I must have known that people died, but it was the first time that I had given it any thought, and it made me sad for days. We were protected in other ways, too. There was a rough element in Cambridge, and probably still is, but they mainly lived on the other side of the Huntingdon Road.

My mother wasn't a fan of housework, but she was a great enthusiast for boosting our education. During our spring and winter holidays, Ann and I went to dancing classes because, at a slightly older age, parties would involve traditional dances like the waltz or the fox trot.

We also played badminton at the Guildhall with other children of our age, and I got private coaching in cricket. But my mother's keenest passion on the educational front, apart from teaching us mathematics, was reading to us, and then encouraging us to read. Every weekend she brought books round to the house, often selecting them on the advice of a friend who was a publisher. My favourites tended to be tales of battles or adventure, often in the fantasy realm like the works of BB or the Lord of the Rings, but I also liked humorous books like the works of PG Wodehouse.

The works of Wodehouse were banned from the house, because they were the only books that my father read, apart from serious works on architecture, and my mother got sick of hearing him talk about them. My elder sister read a lot but didn't take her schoolwork as seriously as my mother expected – which was very seriously indeed!. Education had been my mother's route to a fulfilling life and an escape from her family background.

When I was nine or ten, I was a bit of a dreamer. I thought I would grow up to be a writer. I filled an exercise book with a play, a hundred pages or so long, about a quarrel between the Greek gods. I thought it was terribly clever and funny. It was gibberish, of course, which is often the case when writing flows off the pen – not that I used a pen. I probably used a pencil or a biro. At school, all the desks had ink wells and our pens were sticks, with nibs instead of lollies, attached at the end. One poor boy in my class got himself into endless trouble because he couldn't handle a pen without getting some of the ink over himself, as well as the page he was writing on. He was a boarder too, and possibly dyslexic, so his life must have been a misery in an age that didn't recognise such problems. Life got easier for most of us when we started using fountain pens.

Apart from participating in all the activities organised by our parents, Ann and I spent a lot of our weekends and Easter and Christmas holidays going out with our separate friends. My parents kept open house, and our friends would wander in and out, accepting whatever simple food was on offer. When I was ten or eleven years old, I fell half in love with a pretty girl of my age called Anne Scarisbrick. She went to the same school as my sister Ann, and Ann and I often went round to her house to play cards and board games. At other times we went on walks together, just the two of us. Then one day, Anne Scarisbrick announced in a solemn voice that we weren't allowed to meet any more because one of her mistresses had advised against it. The Perse School for Girls had high standards in those days!

My two closest friends were Chris Smith and Tom Griffiths. Chris was the son of a biology don living further up the Huntingdon road. He wasn't heading in an academic direction himself. Or I assume he wasn't - though sons of of university lecturers had an uncanny knack of growing up to become dons themselves. His interests at that time were not in the classroom, but outdoors. Together we cycled off to the wooded hills at the opposite ends of the town, known as 'The Gogs'. There we entered the beach woods and climbed the trees to pull down dead branches with the aid of a rope. Then we would make our fire, throwing eggs, bacon and sausages into a frying pan and sitting around the fire as we ate our lunch.

More often, even in bad weather, we went fishing. As with all hobbies, fishing required an increasing amount of equipment. The basic stuff I acquired from Uncle Jack, who had left a number of rods propped against the corner of the wall in the small bedroom behind the study where I slept. After that came nylon fishing line, hooks of various sizes, keep nets and maggots, to be used as bait, crawling around inside a tin. I think what I liked most about fishing was sitting idly on the banks of a river in tranquil surroundings, watching my float bob up and down on the water and imagining the silent monsters lurking in the depths below.

Actually, I tell a lie! I really wanted to catch a large fish, like a pike, or a substantial bream, but the looked for event never happened.

Tom Griffith led a more protected life, nurtured by his mother and older sister in one of the large houses occupied by university dons in the leafy haunts of Grange Road beyond the Backs. His father was a classics don, and he was interested in classics himself. We played cricket in the nets erected in a corner of his garden. We both skipped a year together at school and often sat together in class. Tom was better at cricket than me, as he was at everything else. He was nearly a head shorter, with short black hair and a clean and neat appearance, which in some way matched his responses in class. We often went to Fenners together to watch Cambridge University play cricket against the County sides as well as the Australian team with their formidable fast bowlers. But the Cambridge team had some international players too, including the future captain, Ted Dexter. On the day we watched the team bat against Australia, a batsman called James managed to score a century. The headline in the Cambridge Daily News read 'Home, James., and don't spare the Aussies!'

Tom and I spent two years in the top form at St Faiths – a group of precocious, and probably obnoxious, kids in short trousers destined to go on to win scholarships at various public schools. School kids in the fifties were much less open and chatty when talking to adults than most of the kids we meet today. We would raise our caps and smirk and generally behave as if adults belonged to a different world. In my first year in the top form, I came somewhere near the bottom of the class. I was more of an organiser and an instigator – and the only subjects that I enjoyed were classics and creative writing. In my final year, I persuaded my precocious classmates to translate their allotted portions of a Greek play, the Bacchae, which we were currently studying in class and – with the encouragement of Mike Bayon - we put these fragments together to perform the play in front of the parents. I also organised a school newspaper with jokes and cartoons. One of the jokes I was proud of at the time was 'What shall we do with a drunken sailor? To which my answer was, 'Find out what he's been drinking and see if there's any left.' The cartoons of the teachers had captions underneath which read 'Sayings of the Great.' For these, I earned a double-minus for 'misplaced humour' from my geography teacher, which was quietly removed by the headmaster.

Apart from our individual choice of friends, there were the Cambridge families that we all knew. First, there were the Howards. Maurice Howard was the senior master at the Leys, balding and grey-haired when I first met him, though he went on to live to the age of ninety-nine. He was a modest man and, according to one of his sons, it was only the thought of having to attend his 100th birthday celebrations that prompted his abrupt departure from the scene. Many people thought, at the time I attended the Leys, that he should have gone on to become headmaster when the previous one left. He had served as a major in the army, and he was known to be both highly organised and indefatigable in everything that he did - including a great many good works. Our two families were often in and out of each other's houses.

Robert accompanied us on one of our camping holidays, and we have seen a lot of each other over the years. He became an architect and one of his hobbies has been to make countless sketches of famous buildings, including all the Oxford and Cambridge colleges. One subject in which he excelled was geography. Whereas I could get lost in a wood a mile from home and cheerfully set off in the wrong direction, he would look up and assess our position with pin-point accuracy and say, "You can go that way if you want but the house is over there."

Robert is a tall and affable fellow – the kind of all-round sensible person with a dry sense of humour who was made head prefect at my prep school. In our later teenage years we went on a trip to London together and missed the last train home, so we walked from Liverpool Street station to Paddington because I thought we could sleep the night there as the station had padded seats. It didn't. We traipsed back to Liverpool Street to catch the early train. 'Is that train going to Cambridge?' I asked the porter. 'I don't know,' he said. 'It's supposed to, but you can't be sure.' British Rail wasn't any better in those days than its more recent replacement.

Then there were the Taylors who lived in a large house, further up the Huntingdon Road. Elizabeth Taylor I have already mentioned, but she had two older brothers, one of whom, John Taylor, was head boy when I first arrived at the Leys. He looked like just the sort of person who ought to become head boy. He was tall, intelligent and authoritative, in a friendly way and, despite gasping with asthma, performed heroically, propping up the scrum on the rugby field.

Finally, there were the Scotts, who lived just a few blocks down our road. Eleanor Scott was a friend of my mother's from her university days. Mrs Scott radiated a certain energy and magnetism. With Ann and myself, she was a force for good; inviting us round to her house to chat with her sons, Martin and Julian, and participate in her amusing party games. Her husband was a lecturer in mathematics, who wandered around the house in a diffident way, leaving Eleanor to do most of the talking. He once spent nearly half an hour gathering all the apparatus to make me a cup of coffee, and then absent-mindedly drank it himself. I only knew the boys in those days as a pair of spirited ruffians who ran into our house in hobnail boots and climbed over all the furniture. They went to a different prep school, so I didn't really get to know them until they were teenagers and we both went to the same school.

My father had a cousin called Auntie Jane, who featured a lot in my prep school days. She cut the air with her loud, posh voice which she may have acquired since marrying Uncle Jock, whose family owned the mill at St Neots. Uncle Jock looked and sounded like a country gentleman and he had all the accoutrements. He owned a Queen Anne house beside the bridge at St Neots, with what estate agents might call a mature garden, stretching down past the nurseries, the orchard and the donkey paddock to the river Ouse where I was allowed to fish. When Ann and I were first invited to stay, we found the house run with military precision. Meals - which included elevenses - were held at regular times, and then we were pushed out to play in the garden. Ann made great friends with one of their dogs, a black retriever, but we learned later that Uncle Jock felt obliged to shoot it. "It's a game dog, you see," he said in his loud staccato voice. "No use to me once it's been tamed, you see."

The evidence of all this shooting and fishing could be seen and smelt from the rabbits and plucked pheasants hanging from hooks in the larder, visible beyond the kitchen. 'You need to come and fish in my mill pond,' Uncle Jock told me. 'It's stocked with pike and perch, trout – all sorts of fish in that mill pond.' My father warned me that this wished for event was never likely to happen but I was still allowed to take the bus to St Neot's and fish in the river at the end of Auntie

Jane's garden where the gardener tossed bait into the water to attract more roach and perch than I caught in the river Cam.

When I was twelve years old and my brother John – the youngest in the family – was seven, my mother started teaching mathematics at The County High School for Girls and my father's domestic duties increased to the extent that he was only too happy to give me money to buy a picnic and cycle off with my friends to go fishing or make a campfire in the woods and cook bacon or sausages. But as I grew older, I found the pressure to live up to my father's expectations increasingly irksome. He wanted me to be involved in all kinds of useful jobs about the house, like digging up the lawn and laying turf or painting and decorating. I was too lazy and selfish to be interested in these jobs and I wasn't very good at them. My father admired people who were 'good with their hands.' He was jokingly proud of the fact that I opted to study classics instead of maths and science, but he couldn't help suggesting that arty people were a bit superficial and lazy.

Despite harping on about his many failings, he had an enviable range of skills, building a damp course in our house on the Huntingdon Road or cannibalising two second-hand Fords in order to create one viable car – well, nearly viable. You still had to hold the door handle on the passenger side to be sure of a safe ride. My father also did most of the cooking and cleaning, while my mother, full of bright-eyed enthusiasm, cleaned furiously once or twice a year and shopped energetically once or twice a week and, as soon as she started working, spent most of the time in an armchair in the sitting-room preparing her lessons.

It was soon time to move on to the Leys, where I won a minor scholarship. The fees were still significant, though with the scholarship and being a home boarder and my father being a teacher, they were reduced to a manageable amount. As far as I was concerned the most significant change was that I had to wear long trousers, attend the school chapel twice on a Sunday, wearing a blue suit and a stiff collar, and spend most of my free time during the school day in East House; one of the five 'houses' where the boarders slept in dormitories and the home boarders wandered in and out like uninvited guests.

Each house had prefects – older boys who were given a degree of responsibility. I was lucky in this respect because the prefects in my house were two worthies who carried out their duties in a sensible, unassuming way. One of them was Benson, who later became a headmaster, and the other was Martin Bell, who became a BBC war correspondent and then a member of parliament. The boys in my year were another matter. As a confident youngster, fresh from prep school, I asked a large kid with a florid face in my year group, "What's the time please?" and he turned and said, "Time you got a watch!" He looked around for the approval of his peers. I can't remember if they noticed. There was also an Irish boy in my year who walked around with his head in the air and a look of surly defiance, as if to say, "I can do what I want in this place.' He was certainly taller and stronger than any of us in this jungle world, though a year later he was dwarfed in size and status by two much larger boys who starred on the sports field. In a game of hockey, he once aimed a ball from two yards directly at my leg. I met him forty years later at the only Old Boys' dinner I attended, when I was living in Jersey and he was living on the Isle of Man. I asked him in a casual way, "What are you doing nowadays?" and he gave me a blank stare and said, "wondering what you're doing nowadays."

In the space between lessons, we returned to our 'house' which, for a home boarder in a house full of boarders, made it hard to know where to put yourself. Upstairs, there were dormitories and on the ground floor, apart from the small rooms known as 'studies' allotted to the older boys, there was one large space with armchairs round the sides and, in the middle, a full-size snooker table and a table tennis table. Both tables tended to be dominated by the older boys at break times. Downstairs was a room of similar size with our individual lockers attached to the walls, three or four open showers at one end and a large, square, shallow bath in the centre, full of hot water, in which twenty or so boys of all ages could splash around and wash after an afternoon on the sports field.

My first term at the Leys felt like taking a step backwards. Quite a few of the brighter boys skipped the first year and started in the fifth form, but parents who wanted to ensure that this process took effect sent their sons to the school in the preceding summer term. This was the case with Chris Smith. But when I saw him standing on the steps of School House and gave him a cheery greeting, he just looked at me and said 'Don't be gassy!' Being gassy meant having the temerity as a new boy to address anyone above one's age group. This was the traditional way of knocking youngsters into shape. I felt angry and betrayed, but I don't think the feeling lasted that long. We still went fishing together sometimes.

We practised sports on four afternoons a week, returning at four o'clock for an hour and a half of lessons. But on Wednesdays, we were obliged to join the Scouts or the CCF which was the school cadet force. I joined the Scouts for a year until the futility of our activities was brought home to me by the sight of a friend spending most of the afternoon in the scout hut trying to cut a penny in half with an axe. Out of a misguided sense of duty, I decided in the following year to switch to the CCF. I found the CCF gave me an ideal opportunity to discover the full range of my incompetence. Whether it involved finding and then polishing my kit before the weekly inspection, marching in time with the other cadets or remembering to say 'halt' instead of 'stop' to avoid them heading on blindly into a brick wall, I feel that my military career once started was destined for an untimely end. I even failed the end-of-year examinations by whispering 'What's the time?' to a fellow cadet and getting done for cheating.

But sport was another matter. I was in the unusual position of liking sport, but not being very good at it. My parents were not really sporting people either, though my father had won a half-blue at Cambridge in lacrosse and my mother had won a half-blue in netball, so they'd have been happy for me to succeed in this area. I loved cricket but was somewhat lacking in team spirit. I wouldn't have cared which team won if the rules had been altered to enable me to bowl at both ends. I have since developed a lifelong prejudice against Etonians because, several years later, I was invited to make up the numbers in an all-Etonian cricket match, where instead of being asked whether I could bat or bowl, I was simply asked to field in the deep and bat at number eleven. 'What a cricketer they missed in me!', as Nero might have said. However, I did win a medal for cross-country running, chiefly because many of the more likely winners were busy playing cricket. In any case, the effort involved in running gave me piles which lasted about six months and proved not only painful but an assault on my amour propre. But this came later, in my last year at school, in the midst of my A-level examinations.

My best friend in my first year at the Leys was a small boy with round glasses and smooth, reddish hair and a happy disposition called Osborne. In our spare time, we used the school kitchen to boil sugar and butter and syrup and Nestles milk and various other ingredients to produce an exciting range of toffees and fudges. I even suggested that we should put them on sale, but this proposal was frowned upon. I then took my entrepreneurial ideas in a different direction and wrote letters to Ovaltine, Horlicks, Nescafe and Maxwell House explaining that, as a young boy in my first year at the Leys, I had difficulty staying awake during lessons and wondered if their products would provide a cure to this problem. A week or so later, a huge jar of Horlicks arrived through the post, followed shortly afterwards by large tins of Nescafe and Ovaltine. Last to arrive came a letter from one of the managers at Maxwell House. "For a boy of your age," wrote the manager, "the amount of caffeine needed to keep you awake might be dangerous to your health. Instead, I suggest that a brisk run round the school playing field before breakfast would be a better solution."

Like my friend Osborne, I skipped the first year at the Leys and started in form V2A, which meant I got taught physics by my father. I sat at the back, anxious to avoid claims of favouritism, next to a cool and witty older boy called Latimer, who performed in all the school plays and went on to become an actor. He sat at the end of the bench next to the gas mains, which enabled him to turn off the gas every time my father attempted to light the Bunsen Burner. At quite an early stage in my life, my father realised that I was unlikely to become a physicist. He told the class, 'There's a boy at the back of the class who doesn't know how a bicycle pump works.'

My father was fond of illustrating his lessons with cartoon drawings on the blackboard. He once spent an entire lesson explaining the Archimedes principle. He began by drawing Archimedes in his bath, then decided that he needed some Greek attendants – so he chalked them in too – and then thought they must be standing in front of a temple, so a Greek temple appeared in the background. I still can't remember what the principle was designed to prove. But the other boys seemed amused by the demonstration and most of them seemed to understand what Archimedes was on about.

I started off doing badly in Physics on purpose, to escape charges of favouritism, and then found that, even when I tried, I was quite clueless at the subject and glad to be demoted to the B form. I think my father was probably as glad as I was, since he wasn't overly keen on teaching his own son. I eventually opted to take my 'O' levels in General Science, narrowly passing in this watered-down version of the subject, even though my written answer to the question 'How do you turn sulphur into sulphuric acid' was 'Just add water and dilute to taste.'

I shall always think of my father as 'a better man than I, Gunga Din' but he was a man of fixed views - some of which seemed to date from the 1930s. One of the problems that can afflict teachers, as I found from my own experience, is that the act of repeating the same explanations year after year to a series of teenage classes can make one dogmatic. Opinions harden into facts and you can easily forget the need to justify them. As I reached adolescence, I infuriated my father more and more by arguing with him. I think part of these arguments stemmed from a seismic generational split that opened up between the baby boomers born towards the end of the war and anyone born even two years earlier who espoused the moral certainties of the fifties, satirised by Peter Cooke in 'Beyond the Fringe -' though my father found the show funny too when we watched it together in Cambridge before it was performed in the West End, so perhaps I exaggerate.

I was, it must be admitted, quite often a pain in the neck; argumentative, careless and impractical, and prone to teasing. If I felt sorry for myself, my father would rush to my aid, but as I grew older, that wasn't a concession I was willing to make. My father liked to support the underdog, and I didn't want to belong to that species. But it never occurred to me to wonder why Ann and I were criticised and enlisted to help with household chores, while the younger ones were not asked to do anything because they were still regarded as too young to be asked.

Our differences caused a slight rift between us when I entered the wilderness of adolescence, a year after I entered the Leys. Most boys at a boy's public school found love or sex where they could find it, and when my father searched in my chest of drawers and found a love poem I had written about a boy, he reacted with incomprehension and disgust. My homosexual leanings only disappeared – after a fairly long bisexual period – in my first year at university, but my parents' habit of checking everything we wrote in private – for Ann and Sarah committed their thoughts to writing too – added to the atmosphere of tension as we entered our teenage years. My father's voice echoed through the thin walls of the house, and what our parents said in private was often discussed with their colleagues at school. Ann attended the Perse School for Girls, where she suffered from my mother's private conversations with the headmistress. Sarah attended the school where my mother taught, which worked to her disadvantage because my mother got increasingly annoyed with her choice of friends.

My father had an embarrassing temper. His face would go red and his voice would grow shrill and he would proceed to pick your character apart. Then, because he was a kind man, he would always end one of his tirades with an apology which would begin 'Look I'm sorry but...' The problem was that after the 'but', he would remember the cause of his annoyance all over again. Because the Leys was a boarding school, it had ten or twelve buildings scattered over a wide campus – the science block being just one of them – so a week could pass without my bumping into my father at all. But I do remember one occasion, when I noticed a group of boys streaming out of a physics class two hours after their class had been due to end. My father had got so annoyed with them that he slammed the door of the classroom and walked out. Unfortunately, he had inadvertently locked them in.

He spent the rest of the morning taking the door apart in order to let them out – and then apologise, of course!

This wasn't the only door slamming incident I remember. My elder sister Ann was chatty and gossipy and liked going to parties and generally being 'naughty', as she still likes to describe it. As my father's friends and relations were quick to discover, she was a perfectly normal teenage girl – friendly, helpful and full of everyday common sense. This was not as my mother saw it. She went out when she should be at home studying. She was just silly! An altercation erupted one afternoon in Ann's tiny bedroom overlooking the Huntingdon Road. My father hurried up the stairs to find my mother and Ann sitting side by side on the bed exchanging angry words with one another. He started in his painfully logical way to explain why they should make peace with one another. Ann shouldn't speak to her mother like that and her mother should... well, I don't think he got much further than this before he realised that he'd turned their anger against himself. In exasperation, he slammed the door and walked out, only to realise that he'd locked them both in the room. He had to fetch some tools, place a ladder below Ann's bedroom window overlooking the Huntingdon Road, and then climb in and face their mute glares of disapproval as he fiddled with the lock until they were able to leave the room.

This was not the first time my father had been obliged to climb through a window on the Huntingdon Road. There were several elderly widows on our block who were quick to spot his usefulness as a handyman. One of these ladies was so afraid of being burgled that she had to phone to explain that she had succeeded in locking herself into her own bedroom. My father went round to the house with a ladder and a bread knife and I went with him to hold the ladder. After a time, he shook his head and called down to me. "It's no good. I'll keep trying, but you'd better go back and explain to the police that we need their help." I was ten or eleven at the time and, since the only number I knew for the police was 999, I dialled that and said, "There's an old lady up our street locked into her bedroom and my father's up a ladder trying to open her window with a bread knife." I'd given them the essential facts, I thought and, when I opened the front door, I felt pleased to see how quickly they'd responded.

There was one occasion when my father's efforts as a handyman were not appreciated by his immediate neighbours. Next door to us lived the Horgans - an Irish widow who shared the house with her grown-up son. My father took the opportunity of their absence to repair the garden fence. But on their return they were furious and didn't speak to us again for years. In rebuilding the fence, they contended, he had placed it too far on their side and destroyed all their roses. Hostilities were maintained by the Brown children – one of the few occasions when we found ourselves on the same side. When our parents weren't around, we called insults over the fence, and on one occasion, when I was playing cricket, using a piece of brick as the ball, I hit a six to mid-off and it broke one of their upstairs windows, Mr Horgan appeared shortly afterwards at our front door, handed over the brick, and said 'I believe this belongs to you.'

There must have been times in our teens when we seemed to neutral observers like a bunch of children run amok. My father often lost his temper, but his anger just washed over us. He would sit marking homework until one o'clock in the morning and, when he wasn't teaching and preparing lessons, he was often busy ferrying Sarah and my mother to and from school.

I suppose one of the problems he faced was that he didn't get much help from my mother. She was not only a confirmed blue stocking, but she had just started work at a new school and her thoughts were consumed with mathematics. Once she arrived home, she sat in an armchair in the sitting room, surrounded by papers and, if you got too close, she was liable to greet you with wide-eyed enthusiasm and rope you into an impromptu maths lesson.

On the few occasions when I bumped into my father at school, smoking his pipe in the Physics Lab, I got the impression that here was a man at peace, enjoying a rare moment of tranquillity. His conscience simply wouldn't give him a rest, which meant in practice that, when you argued with him, he would always end up by giving in. This was most obviously the case in his dealings with my mother. One of the rules she imposed on him was not to drink alcohol. My mother loved and admired my father, but somewhere in the recesses of her mind lay the image of a naval captain she had met who, because he lived and worked in a culture notorious for heavy drinking, had decided to set an example to his men by becoming teetotal. Later, when my parents started taking camping holidays in France, which lasted well into their seventies, my mother decided that, if the French had wine with their meals, it must be a good thing and – to my father's satisfaction, the rules on alcohol became relaxed and they were both happy to slosh back the red wine over an evening meal. They were shot of their children by then; another source of relief.

My mother also took exception to some of our relations – like Uncle Jack who was rarely invited to the house because he appeared to criticise one of her rare attempts to provide a meal by taking out a packet of Andrew's liver salts afterwards and sharing them with his wife. Poor Uncle Jack! Whether the offence was deliberate, I have no means of knowing. He sent me a Masai sword in a decorated leather sheathe for Christmas and it got treated as an object of extreme danger – as it probably would have been in my hands – and quickly got stowed away out of reach. And every year, on his annual visit from Kenya, he went salmon fishing in Scotland and sent us a huge salmon through the post.

I suppose you could call my family 'shabby genteel' in Orwell's phrase, though my father firmly defined us as lower middle class with certain fixed values, like respecting one's social superiors, 'doing one's bit' and being morally upright. Our differences slowly emerged as I became a sixth former at the age of fifteen, and my views on life, which were inclined to change on a daily basis, differed from the fixed certainties that my father espoused. He was once heard to complain to a colleague that every time I walked into the house, he just had to say to me, 'Pass the salt and make an argument out of that if you can.'

Among more than 500 students aged between 13 and 18, there must have been about eighty home boarders at the Leys, mostly the sons of local academics. By the time we reached the sixth form, some of us – like myself – got so involved in the life of the school that we cycled home quite late in the evening. By this stage, we had mostly established ourselves as sportsmen or academics. The sportsmen were generally regarded as potential leaders, who would go up north and help run the family business or go out and become minor officials in what was left of the British Empire. Given the choice of becoming a sportsman or an intellectual or nobody at all, I had long since decided to become an intellectual.

At the Leys, I was inspired by a young and multi-talented teacher called Derek Baker. Derek Baker had a marvellous stillness and composure about him. He talked in a bright, chirpy voice, listened and offered advice. Although he was a history teacher – a subject I didn't study – Derek Baker achieved most of his successes through one-to-one tutorials. He sent his 'o' level history classes to the library to prepare their essays from the Encyclopaedia Britannica while he sat in his room in School House and encouraged one boy after another to discover his talent in mountaineering, sailing or rowing – or, in my case, writing. I showed him a play I had written, called 'The Keys of Heaven', which he arranged for me to have performed in the school chapel. The theme of the play was that Heaven might not to be to everyone's liking, as a lifetime of religious observance counted for little if true spirituality held no appeal for you.

Noticing that I was interested in poetry, Derek Baker organised a poetry club where a small group of us would meet in his room once a week to read our poems. And, after that, he suggested that I should edit a school newspaper called 'Comment' which would be more daring and outspoken than the school's established 'Fortnightly.'

To return to my family... Until the age of 15, I still thought of my family as among the happiest people I knew. My parents were a friendly and handsome couple, as their many friends often remarked. They kept an open house where my friends dropped in and ate whatever food was on offer. I often cycled home with Julian Scott and we'd have long conversations about life and how depressing we found it all. Julian had become a bit of a teenage maestro. He had an unruly mob of yellowish hair, was a keen physicist and had recently become mad keen on playing the cello, at which he excelled. I think he was more depressed with life than I was, but mostly we were just waking up to a new world of ideas and trying them out on one another.

When our camping days were over, my father arranged an exchange with the Laurent family in France. Monsieur Laurent arrived in April with his daughter, Claude, to start the exchange. He was a short, bullish-looking man with a stubble of grey hairs who stood bolt upright and pronounced his opinions with certainty. His first remark, on spotting the guinea pigs running loose around our small lawn, was that these animals would be good to eat. He smiled as he said it, as if to say, 'There you are! That's what you should do.'

His daughter Claude – a pretty girl standing demurely by his side – proved from my parents' point of view – the perfect guest. And they still retained this view twenty years later, when she had seen off her sixth or seventh husband. It was true, in a sense. She agreed politely to every excursion my parents suggested and seemed quite happy to eat our meals, which in itself was sometimes a challenge. My mother chose the desserts, which were dried bananas – that phase lasted a year – black currents and cream, another year – and yoghurts. I can't remember the yoghurt phase ever ending, but I do remember my mother asking "Ron, would you like a yoghurt?" and his reply, "You know I don't like yoghurts," which worried her not a bit. She just looked up from her plate and said, "Oh! But they're nice!"

Claude sat through these lunchtime conversations with polite interest. She only once showed the mischievous side of her character. And that was on her first visit, when she suggested a game of hide and seek and grabbed me, hiding behind some coats, and gave me a secretive kiss. Alas, this was the only time she really noticed me. Her future boyfriends were all at least ten years older.

Claude was only fourteen when she arrived in Cambridge with her father. It was arranged that the two girls would come to stay for two weeks at Easter while one member of our family would stay with the Laurents for four weeks in August. My turn came one year later. I stayed one week with the family in Paris and the following three weeks in their home in Menton. The first thing I discovered about Paris was the amazing richness and variety of the food on offer in the shops. Occupied France seemed to have recovered much more quickly from the war than England, where even chicken was a rare luxury.

But the moment I arrived, my most amazing discovery was that French was not just a language you learned from a textbook, but a language people actually spoke. Monsieur Laurent sat at the head of the table and stated with assurance, "Donald, L'Angleterre est finie!" and I spluttered to express my disagreement in French, at which point he would say, 'Donald, vous etes jeune, vous devez comprendre que, s'il a une chose qui compte dans la vie – c'est le pouvoir.' In other words, he was an amiable fascist. His position was Chef de Gare de l'Est, and I think his opinions were self-taught, but he and his wife – apart from teaching me to enjoy food, made me an ardent Francophile.

At the end of the first week, we took the train to Menton. The Laurents, since Monsieur Laurent worked for the SNCF, travelled first class, while I sat in a second class compartment squeezed between two French families eating their ham and Camembert baguettes. We arrived at Nice in the early hours of the morning. Then followed the most exciting part of the journey, as the train wove its way along the Mediterranean coast. Through the window on my right, I saw clusters of pink and white villas dotted with orange trees and bougainvillea sloping down to a deep blue sea. And then, on the other side, as we approached Menton, I saw lemon trees too – for which the town is famous - and a distant view of mountains.

The Laurent's house in Menton stood on the Boulevard de Garavan opposite the cemetery, while the road on our side sloped down towards the Italian border. In the morning, you could see the mountains towering in the background and a line of Italians snaking their way into France in search of employment. On the first evening, Claude proposed another game of hide and seek, this time in the cemetery. Years later, I learned from Monsieur Laurent, who laughed about the incident and assumed that I was responsible, that I had made history by forcing the city council to close the cemetery after dark.

Our days followed a familiar pattern. In the morning we would walk down the winding, paved pathway through the old town – much prettier than its neighbour, Monte Carlo, sometimes stopping to buy provisions in the marketplace or sit eating ice creams in the arcade, listening to the Italian singer belting out the popular songs of the day: 'Nel blu di Pinto di blu,' or 'Eenie weenie, yellow polka dot bikini.' Then we would spend the mornings sitting on the rocky beach chatting and taking the occasional swim, or watching well-dressed men strolling up and down the promenade preparing their stomachs for the meals that their wives were preparing back home. Monsieur Laurent kept reminding me that the sun in Menton was not the same as 'en Angleterre.' The heat was literally blistering.

Then we returned for a substantial lunch and Claude was given the money to entertain me for the afternoon. As soon as we were out of sight of the house, a tall Frenchman would emerge from a side street and Claude would inform me that this was her latest 'amour'. They were soon locked in each other's arms, and then continued down the path in heated conversation, with me lagging behind. This young man, a soldier returning from the war in Algeria, was mad about Claude. They all were. This one crashed his car in an attempted suicide when he realised that the romance was doomed. Behind Claude's gentle appearance lay a turbulent thirst for 'l'amour'. 'L'amour' was a popular theme at that time and must have absorbed her every waking thought. This was the heyday of Brigitte Bardot– to whom Claude bore a slight resemblance.

I was sixteen by this time and returned to school fired up by my enthusiasm for France and everything French. I was in the second year of the sixth form by now, studying for 'A' levels in Latin, Greek and Ancient History. In my holidays I got a job working at David's Antiquarian Bookshop. The part I liked best was working at their stall in the marketplace in the centre of town.

Cambridge was a great place to grow up in, especially if you lived on the Huntingdon Road. On the opposite side of the road, as you walked into town, you could veer right at Histon Road and reach 'The Backs'. These were the backs of the colleges visible on the other side of the river Cam, with their extensive lawns reaching to the water's edge. To the right of the colleges lay the leafy homes of the academics. But despite the disparity in wealth, most academics – especially the scientists -were less concerned about status and material possessions than they were about knowledge and academic achievements. The teenagers I met in pubs and coffee bars were mostly the sons and daughters of academics, and they rode bicycles and talked about nuclear disarmament and books and travel ambitions, and very little about cars or clothes. Still, at the back of my mind, I was dimly aware that living in Cambridge was not 'real life' and my private ambition was to explore the world – which in my eyes meant Europe.

But there was another side to Cambridge which probably still exists. On the other side of the Huntingdon Road lay the long lines of grey-brick terraced houses where the townies dwelt, and some of the young townies had developed a resentment against the posh young undergraduates who had come to take over their town. I met a group of them one day when I took another holiday job working at Joe Lyons. I wouldn't say that my days as a waiter were a success. One elderly gentleman beckoned me to his table and asked, "Tell me, young man, do you use that cloth for cleaning the dirty tables or for dirtying the clean ones?"

Lyons was run by two middle-aged sisters with moustaches who looked similar enough to be twins. They once asked me to go up to room 257 and mix some mustard. When I asked for directions, they told me I would find it easily enough because it was the only upstairs room. After half an hour of laborious mixing, I developed a sneeze and realised I'd been mixing pepper instead. At the other end of the room, a lady was using the end of a broomstick to mix soup in a dustbin. I suppose the dustbin must have been clean. After the mustard incident, my next assignment was to work the trolleys that delivered food from the upstairs room to the customers below. Despite my best efforts, I put the trolleys out of action and the queue for food stretched out of the cafe and into the street outside.

I don't know exactly what I did or said to earn the dislike of that group of townies who strolled into Lyons, joking and swearing, but as I opened the door to leave at the end of my shift, one of them stood waiting in the street and pointed a knife at my chest. "I'm telling you this because I like you," he said. "Don't mess with my mate or else he'll go mental." His mate was the gang leader who lived not far from our house. A few weeks later, I was cycling home in the evening along a path that led alongside the river to Silver Street when I found the whole gang blocking my path. My mind rocked with fear. Nobody else was in sight and I had half a second to imagine being knocked to the ground and having fists and boots – and maybe knives – aimed at my body. But just then I heard the same voice say, "Come on, mates. He's not worth it," and before they could change their mind, I sped off towards the lights of town. I had no qualms about not being worth it.

This was the time when I met my first girlfriend, from my sister's school, the Perse.

She was a year older than me and several years more mature. I had actually been to the Perse the year before when they were holding a fete. I won second prize in the fancy dress competition by borrowing a dress from my sister and posing as a Perse girl. The Perse was one degree posher than the County, but many of the dons preferred to send their daughters to the County because the headmistress was known to be more enlightened.

I was awe-struck by my first girlfriend. The first time I went to her house, she led me into the kitchen and I watched enthralled as she made me a cup of cocoa and talked in a very grown-up way about life. Then, as we said goodbye, she leaned forward and gave me a kiss, and I walked home feeling the taste of magic on my lips. The next time we met, as I stood in the dark outside her house expecting a kiss, she reached down and nimbly unzipped my flies. After that, some of the magic was gone, and she became less of a girlfriend and more of a mentor.

I had other girlfriends too – or at least I liked to think of them as girlfriends, though in their case familiarity seemed to rule out romance. A girl who lived further down the Huntingdon Road was a frequent visitor. She was intelligent and attractive and stridently funny, but, when it came to sex, she was always on the lookout for a boyfriend who offered the challenge of the unknown. At the same time, I was in love with a boy a year younger than myself called Robert. This time the love was platonic – from his side, at least - though my parents thought otherwise, and when he came to our house, my mother sat upright in her chair like a startled hen and gave him a sharp stare of disapproval. At school we went on long walks round the grounds, and he was always bringing me gifts of cheese or honey from his father's business. He was a year younger than me, but in many ways kinder and more focussed. While still at school, he earned money, buying and selling antiques, and later became a talented interior designer.

I was preparing for my 'A' levels by now, but relations with my main classics teacher had become increasingly fraught. Mr Southern was a very intelligent man, but I think he must have taken a degree in sarcasm and the fact that he had recently become my housemaster didn't help our relationship. He found me annoyingly careless, as he frequently pointed out.

Fortunately, I had another year in the sixth form and after I had taken my 'A' levels in Classics, I was able to switch to studying for another 'A' level in English literature. This came as a wonderful release. My timetable was reduced to one private lesson a week with an inspiring teacher and all I had to do was to prepare the weekly essay, which often amounted to ten or so pages. My new teacher was also in charge of the CCF and he announced that my future role would be in 'administration' which meant studying in the library. I think I must have read more at this time – or certainly with more enjoyment – than in my entire time at Oxford.

But halfway through the year, after my success in cross-country running, I was stricken with the aforementioned piles. And then came depression. Such are the highs and lows of youth that I looked at myself with new insight and found that I wasn't good at anything – and, more to the point, was certainly not a good person. In these intense moods of depression, even speaking became a difficult exercise. Sometimes a chance word would set it off. And then people would ask why I was acting so dumb, and this made it all worse - until one day, out of nowhere, the cloud would lift again and I would awake with the same cards in my hand but find that they'd suddenly ceased to matter.

I used to have these depressions every few years – which didn't help much when I had a young family and was working as a teacher. But when I arrived in Jersey with the mad idea of setting up a school, these depressions stopped recurring-probably because I was too busy fending off the dangers of financial ruin.

In 1961, I had to prolong my stay at the Leys for an extra term because the scholarship exams took place in October. I chose to apply to Exeter College, Oxford – Oxford because it would mean living away from home, and Exeter because it was high up on my mother's list of approved colleges which weren't too new or dedicated to sport – I can't recall all her other irrational prejudices but she certainly put a lot of thought into the final application process.

I sat my exams in October and was interviewed by an array of dons seated at a long table like wizards familiar to the readers of Harry Potter. There I met my future tutor, Jonathan Wordsworth, whose family owned Wordsworth's cottage and wrote scholarly books on his poetry. He asked me in the typically challenging and instantly recognisable Oxford manner, "You wrote in your exam paper that Keat's poetry is sensuous. Lots of students write that! What an earth does it mean?"

"Sensuous," I replied, "means that it appeals to one or more of the five senses."

"And what about Wordsworth?" he asked.

"I suppose he appeals to the sixth sense," I replied.

At this, the elderly Australian dean laughed and said, "I like this man!" and that was, more or less, the end of the interview. I learned later that I'd been awarded an exhibition and my mother's ambitions were satisfied.

Thus, I had a whole eight months free; perhaps the only time in my life when I might face a similar prospect of freedom. Although I had been a 'home boarder' at the Leys, in my last years at school I became involved in such a whirlwind of activities and friendships that I barely returned home till late every evening. While I was still in the sixth form, my behaviour was tolerated because I was studying for exams – though my father, being a scientist – couldn't quite accept my idea of studying because it involved sitting around, reading a book or wandering off to the cinema. But now, I was permanently at home and most of my friends – being boarders -lived elsewhere. I had to get used to living with my family again.

In my experience, students who leave school at eighteen and go to work in a garage or a bank often become solid, respectable citizens overnight. Their world view is an authoritarian one, shaped by their experience of the school they have left. Students heading for university, on the other hand, enter a second adolescence – a world where they question everything and become a nightmare for their parents to live with. There are exceptions to this rule, of course. Lawyers start talking like lawyers overnight. Medical students, in many cases, follow in their parental footsteps. Scientists are interested in ideas of a different kind. But Arts students learn to question everything and, as I did, sit around arguing with their parents and follow the lifestyle of the time – which in my case was the start of the 1960s; very different from the age my parents grew up in. My father wasn't slow to pick up on my deficiencies. "You are lazy, self-indulgent. You wander round like a tramp, with a cigarette dangling from your mouth," he kept saying. Well, he didn't always use those exact words, but those were the three salient points that featured in his conversation when he was annoyed with me. There were other occasions when he would laugh and joke with me, but these moments were rarer in those days after Christmas when I lounged around in the house with nine months' freedom stretching ahead of me.

My smoking habit had started a year or two earlier. My father smoked a pipe himself, but he kept a silver cigarette box on the sitting-room mantle piece for the benefit of guests. I dipped my hand in the box, lit my first cigarette and soon got hooked on the habit. Julian Scott and his old brother, Martin, would stop at our house on the way home, prop their bicycles against the wall, and I would pass them cigarettes through the window. I spent the next forty years smoking and making desperate attempts to give up. In my first teaching job in a summer language school, I crushed a cigarette on the blackboard and found that I'd been trying to smoke a piece of chalk. And several years later, I told my father-in-law that I had finally managed to crack the habit and he gave a smile of delight. Then I said that I was finding it surprisingly easy and his smile vanished, because I'd unconsciously lit another cigarette.

But the fact that I smoked wasn't my immediate problem when I left school in December 1961. I was leaving a world that had absorbed so much of my time and interest and finding myself stuck at home with my parents, who'd become suddenly immersed in problems of their own. My older sister, Ann, had decided to get married. She thus unknowingly became shackled to a conceited and bullying partner for the best part of forty years. This may not have been an immediate problem for her at the time, but it became a problem for me from a selfish point of view, as it meant - being the eldest sibling at home – that I became the butt of my father's annoyance.

I had recently taken up hitch-hiking, which was quite common in the 1960s. The previous year, my father had bought a VW camper van, which lasted him long into retirement, and my parents took their three remaining children on a touring holiday through Dorset. I must have annoyed them enough to let me part company after a week, and go off hitch hiking through Devon and Cornwall, staying in Youth Hostels and returning home in my own time. The lure of hitchhiking is the excitement of the unexpected, and this experience planted the seed of my ambition to spend my gap year finding a job in Paris and earning enough money to hitch hike to Greece.

Meanwhile, I was stuck in Cambridge, and just unselfish enough to realise that I owed a debt to my family. Being the eldest one at home after Ann's departure, I became the immediate butt of my parent's annoyance. My parents had finally realised that we all had problems. And because in the early 60s any sort of mental problem tended to be ascribed to one's upbringing rather than one's genetic inheritance, they became consumed with worry and guilt. My problem, as my father constantly told me, was that I was lazy and self-indulgent, and I smoked and argued with him about politics or history. What enraged him even more was that my mother sometimes supported me. My brother John spent most of his time after school studying mathematics in his bedroom.

"John doesn't annoy me as much as Donald!" I heard him shouting in a high-pitched voice through the thin walls.

Then there was my younger sister, Sarah, who was 'the pretty one' in my mother's eyes. She was especially anxious about her social life, so every time I went out to a party, or just with a group of friends, I was asked to take Sarah with me – and on my return, my mother would draw me aside to ask how Sarah got on.

John played cards and board games with me, but he didn't talk much and his behaviour just seemed mildly eccentric. When asked to help with the drying up, he spent the entire session drying a single spoon. He once offered to whip the cream and took the jug off to the kitchen, only to return half an hour later with a small square of butter on a plate, which we all found mildly eccentric and amusing. I spent more time with Sarah. I once went to a party with her, where I met an attractive Danish girl who was working as an au pair at the Scotts. We had danced together and the mutual attraction was electric. On the way home, she stopped outside her bedroom window and invited me to climb in with her. The temptation was almost overwhelming, but my sister lagged only a few paces behind and the prospect of getting blamed for deserting her was too awful to contemplate.

I was depressed myself at the time. The thing that depressed me most was that friends kept saying to me, 'You've changed!' In my experience, this is the most negative remark you can make to anyone because it means 'you were once this lively, interesting person we were glad to know and now you're nothing.' I just couldn't fit words into a conversation. I went on long walks, with a cigarette dangling from my lips, nursing my rage at the last uncomfortable argument with my father. But then, for no apparent reason, the mood lifted, and I was able to become sociable again.

My father couldn't understand why I wasn't content to stay in Cambridge and get a job during my gap year. At least we had that idea in common, except that I wanted a job in order to earn enough money to get to Paris. So I found a clerical job at the Cambridge Examination Syndicate, where I worked beside George and Fred in a small office sorting packets of exam papers. George was a mild grey-haired man on the verge of retirement, who had spent the war in a Japanese prison camp. Fred was a lean man in his forties who didn't speak much. One of the supervisors once stopped by and asked George what he was doing. "I'm helping Fred," said George. "And what are you doing?" the supervisor asked, to which Fred said "Nothing." They didn't seem a dedicated workforce at the Examination Syndicate. There seemed to be hundreds of them, crowded into the communal cafe at break times, screwing up bits of paper and chucking them across the table at one another.

I bought into the idea of working and helping my two younger siblings, but I was too romantic or selfish to accept my father's idea of spending my eight months of freedom staying in Cambridge and earning a living. Besides, somewhere at the back of my mind, I knew that my father would always agree in the end, although it made him increasingly angry. So I stayed in Cambridge for two months and earned money, much of which I frittered away until I annoyed my parents to such an extent that they agreed to my idea of going off to find a job in Paris. My father gave me twenty pounds to supplement the meagre amount I had saved. What I didn't realise at the time was that I was far too immature and romantic to survive in the real world outside my own front door without a huge amount of luck. But that turned out to be the secret weapon in my armoury.

I hitch hiked to Dover full of hope and confidence, arriving in Paris with very little cash or knowledge of life, to find a room in the cheapest hotel I could find, opposite the station at Jussieu, on the west side of the left bank. For nearly four weeks, I spent the days walking into shops and bars searching for work, and the nights sitting on the banks of the Seine sharing a bottle of red wine with a young American GI staying in the same hotel, who served in the American army, based on the outskirts of Paris. In a spirit of mutual generosity, he would declare why he liked the British and I would take another swig of wine and mouth some platitude about why I liked the Americans, and then we would share a few disparaging remarks about The French. On one evening, my American friend broke the empty bottle on the quayside and waved it at a group of approaching Algerians who muttered threats and backed away, but I was too drunk to be aware of the danger.

At other times, I walked the streets of the left bank with a kind and gentle Burmese gentleman who worked at the Burmese embassy and led me on a kind of culture tour. He kept stopping to point out sites of historical interest and took me to an old-fashioned music hall where we listened to the songs of Edith Piaf. I read a lot of books during my first weeks in Paris, mostly in French, though I sometimes visited the English bookshop facing across the road to the Seine and Notre Dame. The shop was owned by a descendant of Walt Whitman, who kept open house, while remaining strangely cold and aloof. I saw sleeping figures tucked away behind the books on every floor, including the owner and his wife or mistress. When I asked him for a job, he asked me to stack books on the shelves for a few hours, but the payment turned out to be choosing one of the books.

In search of an evening meal, I sometimes wandered off to 'Les Halles' – the huge marketplace, long since replaced by the Pompidou centre, where fish and meat as well as fruit and vegetables lay waiting on stalls to be sold and loaded onto lorries, and then delivered to all parts of the country. I had it half in mind to hitch a lift on such a lorry. The more immediate attraction of Les Halles was that you could sit surrounded by this buzz of activity in a small café, enjoying a large bowl of steaming hot onion soup washed down with a few glasses of red wine.

But I needed a job and, though I walked the streets tirelessly, stepping into every likely-looking shop or café, the answer was always the same. Britain was not in the Common Market, so you couldn't get a job without a 'Carte de Sejour', which entitled you to live in France long enough to apply for one. In the end I gave up, and placed a small ad in the Figaro, stating 'Young English student seeks any form of temporary employment' - or words to that effect. My first respondent was a sweaty and thickset English journalist who invited me to meet him in a bar in Montmartre and said that he needed a housekeeper. Without specifying exactly what a housekeeper was supposed to do, he led me to a ground floor apartment close to Folie Bergere, smelling of incense and unwashed bodies. To the journalist's irritation, as soon as I entered the sitting room, an elderly man with flowing white hair, dominated the scene. Seated on a chair that resembled a throne, he greeted me with a theatrical gesture and invited me to take a seat and hear what he had to say. He turned out to be a retired actor who dabbled in the occult. He treated me to a survey of my past lives, deciding – rather predictably –that I had once been an Egyptian official working on the pyramids and after that, a Roman centurion.

At this point, the journalist emerged from his bedroom in his vest and pants and grumpily announced that it was time to come to bed. I excused myself, explaining that I needed to go to the toilet, which was conveniently placed next to the front door, opted for the door instead and made a run for it.

My next job offer came from a sober, clean-shaven gentleman from the middle-east who wanted me, in his words, to 'tidy up' his house in the country over the weekend. He would pay me six francs a day and supply me with food. I had a hangover when I met him the next day and sat beside him in his Deux Chevaux as we drove in the pouring rain through the suburbs of Paris. Once out in the country, his car stalled, and I had to get out and push, nearly vomiting as I did so. When we finally arrived at his small country villa, fenced off from similar houses on either side, this polite but unsmiling gentleman gave me precise instructions on what I should and should not do. The small garden was on a steep slope; at the bottom of the slope was a large shed full of assorted furniture and junk. The junk had to be placed in a skip at the side of the house. The furniture had to be cleaned and tidied. The flower beds on either side of the lawn were hideously overgrown and strewn with junk too.

The junk had to be added to the skip, and the tangle of weeds had to be placed on the compost heap at the bottom of the garden. At this point, the gentleman showed me the kitchen and handed over the food, which I was supposed to cook for myself over the weekend. He then explained the heating arrangements. The electricity was on a meter and would cut off at night. He would know immediately if I attempted to adjust the meter. With these parting words, he got into his car and disappeared, leaving me to endure two days and nights of utter loneliness.

The nights were the worst because, just as I was about to go to sleep, the meter seemed to come to life and give a strange buzzing sound, as if someone were trying to make a phone call. I thought about the possibility of burglars trying to case out the house, and I made a dash for the phone, which I never succeeded in finding. Then, when I returned to the bedroom, the buzzing noise would begin all over again. Among the books that I discovered in the house, I found one by Anatole France which I read when I couldn't sleep. The theme was very similar to that of Oscar Wilde's 'Dorian Gray'. Because of the loneliness of my situation at that time, the last words on the fate of the hero are indelibly printed on my memory "...il est devenu si laide, qu'en passant le main sur son figure, il sentit sa laidure."

Friday and Saturday went by in utter solitude, pushing the wheelbarrow, loaded with junk or weeds up the steep slope, and restoring the shed and the flower beds into perfect order, which the owner was able to approve as he stood with his wife – or mistress – when he arrived on the Sunday morning. Whether he was satisfied or not, I have no means of knowing. He remained as impassive as he had been at our first meeting. He simply paid me my wages and drove me back in silence to the hotel in Jussieu.

The final response to my advertisement in the first weeks of my stay came from a family in Aumale, a small village in Normandy, who wanted me to tutor their two children in English, for an hour a day each, over the Easter holidays. I set off on the train with hardly any money and discovered as I sat in the carriage and searched my pockets, that I had lost the name and address of the family. Luckily, very few passengers got off the train at Aumale and a charming, slim and sophisticated lady spotted me immediately as the English student who was due to teach her children. She couldn't have been kinder. Her first action was to lead me into a café and ply me with coffee, croissants, and cream buns. Her hospitality followed a similar pattern throughout my stay. After an ample breakfast, we stopped for coffee and croissants at eleven, a delicious lunch at one, more snacks at teatime and a three-course dinner in the evening. I wish I could say I returned the favour by drumming some English into her two children, but their chief interest was in their two horses that proudly tossed their heads as they pranced up and down the field beyond the hedge at the bottom of the garden. I was persuaded to mount one of them once, and it broke into a gallop and threw me off, to the disgust of the elder son, who was home on leave from the army.

They were a traditional county family. The sons were destined for the army and their daughters were brought up like English debutantes to become wives and hostesses. They were fond of dancing and riding to the hunt, but they treated me very generously and I had an uncomfortable feeling at the end of my stay that I had done little to earn my hospitality and wages.

On my return to Paris, I was offered a job on low wages working in a factory. But I needed a Carte de Sejour. That meant I had to queue up for two days in the courtyard of the Palais de Justice along with other immigrants like the Spanish and Portuguese to apply for the 'Carte de Sejour'. At the end of the second day, after standing two days in the queue, I discovered that I wouldn't be able to receive the card without written permission from my parents.

At this point I was joined for a short time by two friends from school, which meant that I, as the one who had been there longest and picked up a bit of French in the process, led them on the search for a new hotel for the three of us. We found a hotel off Boulevard St Germain, offering a room with three beds for a shared rent of ten francs a night. I had also met an American lady living in a very posh flat in the Ile de France overlooking the Seine, who needed someone for unspecified help, which included getting up early in the morning and taking her seven-year-old son to school. Since the flat belonged to James Jones, the author of 'From Here to Eternity', I imagined that this lady might have money to burn and the help she required might extend to my two school friends too. Had I been more familiar with the effects of drug addiction, I might have noticed something unnatural about the luminous intensity of this lady's light blue eyes. On a more practical note, after the first few days of walking her son to school, I began to wonder when and how much I was going to get paid for my services.

Things came to a head at the end of the first week, when the lady decided to hold a surprise birthday party for her son. This was something I felt my friends could participate in. On the day in question, we all trooped round to the large, expensively furnished flat, keeping well clear of the two monstrous cats – of some rare and unfamiliar species – and hung balloons and paper chains, while the lady went off to collect her son. As the afternoon wore on, my friends grew increasingly suspicious. Being better judges of character or simply more experienced than myself, they began to express their doubts about whether we were going to get paid. It was early evening by the time the lady arrived and the only guest at the birthday party was her son. I don't think she had realised that a surprise party doesn't need to come as a surprise to the guests too.

My friends didn't stay long in Paris. One of them had a father who worked in the Prudential and was able to organise a job for his son through connections in Paris. The other had come over for a bit of a holiday and went back home at about the same time. It was April by now, and I had been nearly a month in Paris, still without finding a job for more than a few days at a stretch. So, with funds running out, I went in search of the cheapest hotel I could find. I trawled the left bank until I found the 'Hotel des Canettes' near St Sulpice and La Rue De Rennes. It was run by two eccentric, elderly sisters who answered enquiries from the open hatch in their bedroom on the second floor which, as far as I could see, only contained a double bed and a parrot in a cage. They offered me a room on the fifth floor, large enough for a single bed and a washstand supporting a basin and a large jug of cold water. The toilet was a hole in the floor a good deal higher up, but you had to supply your own toilet paper. The rent was three francs 50 centimes a night. A perfect arrangement!

It was not long after this that, as I wandered through the streets in the direction of the Seine, I met a fellow who looked about my age – I think he was Dutch or Norwegian – carrying an empty red sack bearing the insignia emblazoned in white 'The New York Times International Edition.' We chatted for a bit, and I asked him "How did you get this job? Don't you need a 'carte de sejour?'" It turned out that 'The New York Times' was allotted a certain number of permits and it didn't matter whom they chose to employ. "Hey! I'm leaving tomorrow!" said the guy. "You can take my place tomorrow if you want."

Suddenly my luck had turned. All I had to do was to walk across the Seine to La Place de L'Opera, go a few yards up the street on my right past the Opera House and collect my batch of newspapers from a friendly, unassuming American who explained that the terms were 15 francs a day, plus 20 centimes for each paper I managed to sell. If you sold a hundred papers a day, this would have amounted to a fortune in today's money, so I guessed the papers wouldn't be that easy to sell. My station, I already knew, would be outside the Louvres – not the museum as it is today – but the old Louvres without the fancy glass frontage.

I walked back past the Opera towards the rue d Rivoli and the Louvres with some trepidation. As I approached the museum, I tried out my sales pitch 'The New York Times, the best paper in America!' and the sound came out as a strangled croak. Below the steps leading into the museum, I found two or three green metal chairs. Standing by one of them, was an Algerian, who greeted me with the feeble leer of the dishonest and downtrodden, and showed me his wares which were cards depicting nude statues from the Louvres – the addresses on the back were doubtless of more interest to potential clients. I placed my sack of papers on a chair and looked around me.

Middle-aged Americans on coach tours of Europe were easy to spot. Most of the men tended to have a curious bow-legged walk as if they had just stepped down from a horse – though they'd probably just spent too long sitting in coaches. These were the vanguard of mass tourism, and it was too easy for snooty Europeans to make fun of them. They were just the first nation with the money to make tourism a popular option, not something to be reserved for a cultural elite. And I noticed that a lot of the middle-aged men were less interested than their wives in the cultural delights of the Louvres. So I read them the baseball scores. And some of them looked up and liked my British accent and paid their 50 centimes for a newspaper. I realised over the next few days that I had chanced on the best spot in the whole of Paris for selling American papers. The Louvres was the Sargasso sea for the great mass of American tourists who started their one week coach tour at the Places des Pyramides, where the Louvres was their first port of call. What's more, they liked my British accent. So it was not entirely surprising that, when I finally announced that I was leaving, I was awarded a bonus for 'early pick-up and quick sales.'

This did not mean that selling papers was easy. At the end of a typical day, I would usually have sold about twenty papers, some of which proved useful as toilet paper at the Hotel des Canettes. After that I would wander up the Champs Elyssee and stop outside popular hotels like the George Cinq and sell a few more, then back to the hotel via the Café Des Deux Magots, where I could always find the odd tourist drinking coffee at Hemingway's favourite café. I even strayed as far as Le Sacre Coeur in Montmartre, where the painters sold their works to wandering tourists and beggars sat beside their bowls pleading for cash. Later, as I grew more confident, I would step onto the coaches before the passengers disembarked before the Louvres and read out titbits of news. On the day that 'Willy Mays hit a homer' – a baseball term that I still don't understand – I sold all my papers before lunch.

I discovered later that selling papers outside the Louvre was illegal, but this wouldn't have mattered in my case, because I was joined after a few days by a middle-aged policeman who came and sat beside me and showed me his copy of 'The Daily Mail' which he was using as his sole English textbook. My job was to explain the difficult words which he had underlined, after which he would thank me politely and wander off.

The Algerian card-seller trusted me enough after a few weeks to hand me his sack to look after while he wandered off for a drink. I left my station shortly after to buy a snack for lunch. I had placed my purse in the sack and when I paid for my sandwich, I reached in the sack for the purse and some of the naughty cards fell over the counter. I didn't wait to see the lady's reaction. I quickly replaced the cards in the sack, took my change, and hurried out of the shop.

I had some interesting encounters with American tourists. An American doctor offered me five dollars – a significant sum – to show him three items of interest in the museum; the Mona Lisa, the Winged Victory and the Rubens room. Since all these attractions lay within easy reach of the entrance, his demands were quickly satisfied, though he spent some time in the Rubens room getting quite excited about the medical condition of the overweight Rubens beauties. The future president Nixon visited the Louvres at one point. Although he had just lost an election to Kennedy, he had no detectable secret service presence. He just walked up the steps with his wife like any normal tourist.

But most of the Americans I met, and chatted with, were students – mainly from Harvard - who were intrigued by the idea of an English student selling American papers in Paris. Their idol was a slightly older student called Nick Suter, who had some connection with the Kennedy clan. He certainly mixed in their circles and assured me that Bobby Kennedy was the clever one. He bent at the knees when he walked, due to an accident in free fall diving, and his younger companions were in awe of him. He once offered to drive me to Rome in his red Ferrari, assuring me that we could get there and back in a couple of days. I rather awkwardly declined the offer because I didn't want to risk losing my job.

Another Harvard student called Michael Able joined me for lunch at the North Vietnamese restaurant, one metro stop from the Louvres. There was a South Vietnamese restaurant too, only a few yards away, but it was generally agreed that the North Vietnamese one was cheaper, though the service was ruder. When I told Michael that my ambition at the end of the summer was to hitchhike to Greece, his eyes lit up and he said 'Hey, you must come on my parents' yacht! We've booked a yacht for a week in August – leaving the harbour in Athens for a tour of the Greek Islands.' I took his address and details, which I quickly lost, and thought no more about it.

However, I did still harbour the ambition of hitch-hiking to Greece. And in August, when my parents came over to stay in a campsite in the Bois de Boulogne, I left my job selling newspapers and went over to join them at their campsite as the first step on my journey. My father was not a fan of hitch-hiking but did not protest too strongly, partly because my mother decided that this was something that young people did. Britain was a bit ahead of Europe in this respect, or some might say more decadent. Scruffy English youths sleeping rough or busking their way through Europe were regarded with horror by the middle-class Austrians, Italians and French, whose sons and daughters still dressed smartly and went to traditional dances, as we did in the fifties. The working class who struggled to find the money to look presentable regarded the scruffy English youths with contempt.

My parents dropped me somewhere on the outskirts of Paris, which was a much smaller city in those days – not very different from the tourist city familiar to tourists today; the central core of three million citizens encircled by a system of motorways that divides them from the ten million citizens living in the suburbs beyond. Hitching a lift wasn't as easy in France as it had been in the UK at that time because the general view of Britain reflected in the French press was of a country in decline, with long-haired Brits freeloading on the soaring French economy. Besides, it was widely believed that accepting a hitch-hiker would jeopardise your insurance claims. However, as I didn't have long-hair and didn't look very threatening – more like a sixteen-year-old high school student of an earlier generation, I was picked up after an hour or so by an amiable Belgian professor and dropped off southwest of Paris somewhere in the region of Tours. I should add that I also must have looked a bit effeminate at that time, which is why I had to decline his offer to share a tent with him.

I wandered off the road and found an idyllic spot at the edge of the woods. I leaned back on my rucksack and gazed down the slope at a meadow ending in what looked like a school, or perhaps a monastery.

Suddenly, a line of schoolgirls in black uniforms followed their teacher into the meadow and proceeded to sing. I have no idea what they were singing, but their voices filled the soft summer air with an enchanting melody, and as I lay and listened, I felt a moment of unadulterated joy that lasted until late in the evening when I pulled out my sleeping bag and went to sleep.

My next stop was Chalon sur Saone on the way to Switzerland. My parents had camped there the year before and had struck up a friendship with the lady who owned the site. I had noticed from previous experience that the French loved my parents. First of all, they made every effort to speak French, which is very important in France. Secondly, they were very appreciative of French food. And finally, my father, with his sense of humour, reminded them of one of those eccentric characters in an old Ealing comedy. Thus, the lady remembered 'Monsieur et Madame Brun' and found me a place next to the water mill where I slept to the sound of rushing waters.

The next day, I was in Switzerland. Hitch hiking was difficult in Switzerland, partly – I suppose – because it was not a very Swiss thing to do, and partly because roads branched off or wound round mountains, so it was never quite clear where the would-be passenger wanted to go. I got two lifts – on both occasions with middle-aged ladies – and headed south towards Ascona on the way to Italy. Here, in the early evening, I was picked up by two cheerful Zoology students from Zurich who told me, as I sat in the seat behind them, that behind me, separated by a steel partition, was a large bear that they were taking over the border to the zoo in Turin. It felt like a great adventure, racing down the Simplon pass into Italy with two talkative and interesting students and a bear for company.

From Turin, I headed west and spent the night in Trieste on the borders of Tito's Yugoslavia. Here everything changed. The newly built road, which ran through Slovenia and Croatia to Belgrade, consisted of large square blocks of concrete on which cars and lorries passed fairly frequently. But the lorry drivers seemed reluctant to stop and most of the cars were small and overloaded with passengers. At one point, two policemen approached – not to arrest me, but to ask if I needed some help. They stopped the next lorry and ordered him to give me a lift. The driver seemed obliging enough, but, as soon as the police were out of sight, informed me that this was as far as he was willing to take me. It was early evening by now and I looked around the flat landscape and saw a path on my right leading to a village where I hoped to buy something to eat. Getting away from the main road felt like taking a step back in time, where villagers tilled the fields and lived in the same way as they had done for centuries. I was greeted with gestures and squeaks – which would have probably made sense to a student of Slavonic languages and led me to the stone cottage belonging to what appeared to be the head man. He greeted me warmly and plied me with home-made bread and wine, talking all the time in a language I had no hope of understanding. I made enthusiastic gestures of gratitude, shook hands, and went my way.

I did get a lift at last, that took me as far as Zagreb, the capital of Croatia, After that I spent a whole day on the road from Zagreb to Belgrade, looking at the passing cars crammed with locals and gazing at the flat expanse of fields on either side stretching as far as the eye could see. Many of the fields were filled with watermelons. I ate one and have never been able to eat another again.

Finally, towards the end of the day, I was picked up by a young German tourist heading for Athens in his shiny blue volkswagen. As far as I could see, Germans in the early sixties had no idea of the horrors they had inflicted on the rest of Europe. They were just proud of the way they had managed to rebuild their country. When the allies moved in after the war, they tried a few war criminals – the ones who hadn't fled to South America – but they kept the old guard in place, because they were the only ones in a position to run the country, and they allowed the large firms like Krupps and Siemens, whose profits were partly derived from slave labour, to continue to operate. It was not until Schmidt took over in the seventies that the horrors of Auschwitz and Dachau were taught to high school and university students. In my first teaching job in Brighton in 1968, an enthusiastic young German teacher told me, "We like the British because during the war you were fair, and we were fair!"

The young German who gave me a lift had a similar mindset. He was rightly proud of the way his generation – admittedly with the aid of American money – had performed an economic miracle, but he was contemptuous of countries like Tito's Yugoslavia, which was so obviously backward in terms of material progress. He kept stopping to ask me to take photos of himself standing in front of one of the numerous potholes in the road. "When I show this to my folks at home," he kept saying, "they will laugh!" In a gross act of ingratitude on my part, I am ashamed to say that, when the photos were developed, his folks would be unable to admire the potholes because the view would be obscured by close-ups of his ample posterior.

He drove me through Yugoslavia and on into Macedonia and down into Greece, by which point it became obvious to him that we were unlikely to become soulmates. My behaviour wasn't helped by the fact that I spent the first night in a shared hotel room suffering from intermittent bouts of vomiting. But he dropped me off, two days later, at my request, at the temple of Sunium overlooking the sea, a few miles from Athens. We said our muted goodbyes, and I pulled out my sleeping bag and slept beside the temple, where Byron had carved his initials on one of the columns.

In the morning, I found a taverna and ate my breakfast of bread and Nescafe, supplemented by a bunch of grapes. Some villagers on the other side of the square stared at me and made pushing movements with their hands, as if to tell me to move off. I suspected from their smiles – and the fact that gestures are not the same in every part of the world - that they were inviting me to join them, so I stood up, then hesitated and sat down again.

Since leaving Paris, I had already had two dangerous encounters that might have put an end to my journey. On the way across Italy from Turin to Trieste, I had been given a lift by a young man on a motorbike, who veered off the route and sped up a long, winding lane which led to a village in the hills where he stopped in a deserted street, pointed a knife at me and demanded money. I gave him a few coins, which – to my surprise - he accepted and rode off again. The second encounter – which seemed innocuous at the time – might have ended my journey. It happened when I stopped in Zagreb, my first port of call in Yugoslavia. I was accosted by a smiling drunk who greeted me warmly, threw his arms around me and said, "You English, very nice," before stumbling away in a hurry. Before he had got very far, I felt a lightness in my pockets and realised that my passport and wallet had gone. I raced after him and had the good fortune to find that two burly policemen had blocked his path. One of them held the man by the scruff of the neck and cuffed him. Then he rounded on me and asked, "Why you speak with this silly man? You can see he is no good." His colleague handed me back the stolen items and nodded agreement, and they walked away – taking the man with them.

When I reached Athens, worse was to come. I found cheap dormitory lodgings close to the Parthenon in The European Hostel where I met an Irishman seven years or so older than myself. We sat drinking retsina – a white wine with a distinctly sour taste – my former classics teacher said that it tasted like bicycle oil, but I doubt whether he had put the comparison to the test. My friend suggested that this would be a good time to visit the Parthenon, because at night you could get in for free. I later discovered that his inspiration had come from reading the works of Lawrence Durrell. All you had to do was climb the Acropolis, though not by the official route because that was closed in the evening. The Acropolis is quite a steep hill, but we were helped by the fact that some workmen had conveniently left a ladder to help us over the last and steepest part of the climb. After a short struggle, we stood gazing up at the Parthenon and down at the actors in a Greek play being performed in the theatre below. I was especially enthralled, because having read the plays of Sophocles and Aristophanes and co. in the sixth form under the guidance of this same sarcastic teacher of Latin and Greek – 'Please sir? What's a mistress, sir? Halfway between a mister and a mattress! Carry on translating!' - here I was at the centre of Greek culture, standing and observing the whole thing in action. What's more, the scene around us was so well lit! It only occurred to me later that the lighting was coming from searchlights, which soon became focussed on two young men illegally treading on sacred ground.

A harsh voice broke the silence: "Halt! Morgen Mort!" I suddenly became aware of this small, optimistically trilingual policeman walking up the slope, pointing a pistol at us. Although we had both had too much to drink, in the dim recesses of my brain I realised something awful might be about to happen. The suspicions of this policemen focussed more on my colleague than myself, perhaps because he was older, or more probably because he was Irish, which the policeman confused with Turkish. But the alcohol was beginning to wear off, and I knew we were in trouble.

He led us a short distance to a small well-lighted police station, where we were placed in separate barred cells facing the main room where a group of policemen talked among themselves, presumably discussing our fate. Thankfully, Greece at this time was a well-run democracy – not the dictatorial regime of the colonels which came later– and the first person to address us was a well-dressed tourist lawyer who said in impeccable English 'The police are wanting to know why you did this stupid thing.' I said, truthfully enough, 'because I studied Greek at school and standing beneath the Parthenon was romantic.' After the lawyer had explained my answer to the police, the whole temperature of the room changed. The policemen began laughing among themselves and one of them offered me a cigarette. Then the lawyer explained that all we had to do was return to our hostel under a police escort and show him our passports. After that, we were free to go. So the three of us boarded the bus together, each paying his own fare, and – once the policeman had checked our passports – the incident was forgotten.

The next day I hitchhiked to Delphi with a Greek farmer transporting pigs to market. Hitchhiking in Greece was comparatively easy. I found the people friendly and curious, and the peculiar geography of the country has caused them to become great travellers. Many Greeks live on islands – and even if they live on the mainland, they are never far from the sea. Communications on land are rendered difficult by the mountainous terrain, so from ancient times onwards their first contacts with their neighbours as well as the world beyond were by sea. At the same time, their first loyalty is not to their country but to the place where they were born and bred, whether it is an island or a particular city or land-locked region.

Delphi is a magical place. It stands at 'mesomphalos geis', the classical Greek term for 'the navel of the earth'; an appropriate site for a holy place where, two thousand five hundred years ago, Greeks would go to consult the oracle. I particularly remember the circular remains of a temple surrounded by mountains, with eagles hovering overhead just as they did all that time ago. This is the first thing you see as you travel up the steep slope towards the small town. It was just at this site, thirty or so years later, shortly after the Falklands war that, returning to this spot with my wife on a warm February evening, we experienced a magical moment. We met a young, attractive Argentinian lady, standing alone in the ruins and gazing up at the tall columns stretching towards the clear blue sky. As we got talking – and she seemed eager to talk to someone – we discovered that she had arranged to meet her boyfriend in Greece but he hadn't turned up. She wasn't in tears. She had probably progressed beyond that point. She had realised that he had deserted her. We invited her to join us at a restaurant – the place we found on the main high street turned out to be run by a Greek who had lived in New York – and I hope we cheered her up a bit, but we parted at the end of the evening, and I have no idea what became of her.

I didn't spend long in Athens after that first trip to Delphi, because – strolling through the streets one evening – I bumped into Michael Able whose address I had lost a month ago in Paris. "Say, aren't you coming?" He asked. "You'd better make your mind up quick, because we sail tomorrow morning!"

Early the next morning, as I gazed up at the huge yacht anchored in the Piraeus, I knew I was stepping into a different world. I was greeted by Michael's parents, a small man tanned by the Greek sun standing beside his wife, who wore a leopard skin bikini. Beside him stood a larger man and his wife who, I later learned, had been invited on this seven day trip round the islands as a consolation for having just lost their only son. Both couples were millionaires; we would probably call them billionaires today. Behind them stood a large, sulky looking teenage girl. I later learned that she didn't want to go on this trip one bit – she wanted to be back in Chicago with her high school friends – though her father kept reminding her that it was costing him a hundred dollars a day. Behind this family group, I spotted seven or eight sailors in smart white uniforms busy on the riggings and a man in a suit who turned out to be the guide. He treated me with barely concealed contempt as I got to know him – I was clearly a freeloader on an expensive holiday while he had to work for his pay.

But Americans have a great way of making you feel at home. They didn't pretend to be anything other than ordinary people enjoying a break away from their country. Life on board followed a familiar pattern. My bedroom was 'the pink room', luxuriously furnished, and I would walk along the corridor in the morning to be served breakfast on a large square table which slanted to remain in a horizontal position as the boat tilted with the waves. Breakfast involved every luxury you could imagine – melons and moussaka and every kind of cereal, along with bacon and eggs and sausages. The yacht travelled mostly overnight and, as we ate breakfast, the guide would enter the dining room and regale us in perfect English with the delights of the next port of the call. Then we would take a dip in the sea, and sit chatting on deck, drinking cocktails, as we prepared for another luxurious meal.

I talked a bit with Michael's dad and his colleague. The colleague was in an understandably sad and reminiscing mode. He once referred casually to 'when I made my first million' – a sum he lost in the great depression and presumably recovered soon after. His wife expressed her sadness in a different way by her kindness to another young man of similar age. She took all the clothes I wasn't wearing and brought them back to me, all washed and pressed. I spent a lot of the time chatting with Michael's sister who wasn't any fun at all, because she was angry with her parents for dragging her away from parties with her school friends at home. When I talked with her, I felt I was in some way paying for my keep. Michael himself didn't speak much. I think he too would rather have been back in Harvard with his friends.

Our first stop was Amphipolis, below Corinth on the shores of the Peloponnese, where Michael's mother, who was something of a patroness of culture at home, ran down the stone steps of the circular, centuries old Greek theatre in her leopard skin bikini, and called "Say can you hear me?" – to prove the wonder of the acoustics.

After that, we set out across the Aegean in the general direction of Turkey. We stopped at Mykonos and Seriphos and Delos – where the Greek city states stored their treasures in separate marble edifices – and we slowly wound our way back to Athens, stopping at other islands whose names I can't remember. On our last lunch together, Michael's father invited us all to make a speech about our experience on the journey. When it came to my turn, instead of saying all the nice things I should have said about his family and their wonderful hospitality, all I could come up with was "Well, I've hitched a lot of lifts, but this was the best lift by far!" Fortunately – as they were generous people – this was greeted with laughter and generous applause.

And that was it. I was on my own again – standing beside the road and hitchhiking my way from the outskirts of Athens towards the Peloponnese. I stopped at Argos to admire the lion gate constructed by the legendary king, Agamemnon, and moved on to Nauplia where I had enough money – or thought I had – to spend a couple of nights in a hotel. I spent a most of the time swimming or sitting reading on the shore, a few steps away from the hotel, enjoying my freedom. This must be a spoilt and ungrateful thing to say, but the hospitality of the rich can pall on you after a while. The wealth is not yours, and the price you have to pay is the freedom to wander off and explore the world and meet interesting people along the way.

However, two days later, I would have gladly given anything to be back on that boat because, when I searched my pockets, I found I had less than the equivalent of about six pounds left - hardly enough to cover the voyage from Nauplia on the east coast to Petra in the west of the Peloponnese. This was where the ferry made the crossing to Brindisi on the southern tip of Italy. Here I had the most extraordinary luck. My first and only lift was a lorry that took me all the way to Petra where I learned that the weekly ferry was due to depart in one hour. After paying for my ticket, I had only four pounds left – perhaps forty in today's money - to see me through until I reached Calais where I could still use my open return ticket to Dover.

The boat was crowded with families and livestock, including goats and chickens. I shifted place from time to time to escape the amorous attentions of a Greek sailor, until I managed to wedge myself securely between two peasant families and their children when, as the night closed in, he finally gave up the chase.

In Brindisi my luck ran out. I walked for hours beside a busy main road reeking of traffic fumes until I finally got a lift to the industrial town of Bari. There, a little way beyond the town, I met a young Italian soldier. We stopped and chatted for a bit and, as the night was closing in, and I explained where I was heading, he mentioned that he had a hut that he wasn't using where I could sleep if I liked. He led me to the hut, I thanked him, and as soon as he was gone, I stared at what looked like an extended ironing board which stood about four feet off the ground. It was about a third the width of a normal bed and, once I managed to climb up and lie on it full length, I spent a sleepless night wondering what would happen if I fell off.

The next morning my luck returned. A lorry driver stopped and drove me all the way to Turin. There he led me into a bar, bought me a coffee and we said our goodbyes. From Turin, I avoided Switzerland this time and headed for Chambery, the other side of the French border. I was dropped off in a village in the mountains on the Italian side of the border. Very few cars passed this way and, as I stood there in the freezing cold, knowing it would get dark soon, an Italian lady emerged from a nearby house and ran up to me. "Scuzi, non insulto?" she asked, and shoved a jacket into my hands. I wanted to say "You bet I am not insulted! I am overwhelmed by your kindness." I think my expression showed it.

I can't remember exactly how I reached Paris, but I had just enough money left to use the metro to navigate my way to some northerly point on the periphery where I was able to stand on the side of the road and hitch a lift. I was lucky enough to hitch one almost immediately with a British journalist who was heading in the same direction. We continued chatting on the boat and parted when we reached Dover. I can't remember the last part of my journey except that I finally arrived at our house on the Huntingdon Road, with a sense of laddish triumph, on the trailer at the back of a van. Thinking about my adventures, and glossing over all the help I had received along the way, I felt confident and mature. All that was to change within one month of arriving in Oxford.

First year students at Exeter College were given a year in college. In their second year, they had to find digs elsewhere. My room mate was a bright young history student from a Liverpool grammar school. In retrospect, he was probably placed with me because he looked as young as myself. The existence of grammar schools – whether or not you approved of segregation at the age of eleven – meant that their students received the same privileged education as public school boys, though with more focus on academic achievement, and consequently outnumbered them at Oxford and Cambridge. The social differences between the two groups were wafer thin, but, being British, we were acutely aware of them. My room mate, Dave, who turned out to be a brilliant history student, was a home loving lad with a steady girlfriend, who was astonished by my ignorance of popular music. The other students I met on my first day were the three other members of our English Literature group - a friendly fellow called John Armstrong, who was always kind and polite but despite his fastidious manners spent most of his free time training in the rowing eight. I spent more time with Harvey Webb, a vicar's son, but a bit of a public school tearaway. I didn't see much of the third student, Henry Quinn, who came from a northern grammar school.

Being a new boy can be a daunting experience, but coming from an academic family in Cambridge, I should have been more suited than most to becoming an Oxford student. The two cities are of similar size and have a similar number of colleges - in my day, thirty or so men's colleges and three or four ladies' colleges. The deficit on the ladies' side was made up for by the number of language schools and secretarial colleges; from which you can guess that in the early sixties, you needed to have enlightened parents and be exceptionally bright to be a female university student.

Teaching – on the Arts side, at least – consisted of writing a weekly essay for a one- to- one tutorial and attending non-obligatory lectures. Since I had spent my last year at school preparing a weekly essay for my English teacher, the transition should have been easy. In fact, I made things simpler by deciding that, since lectures mostly consisted of listening to lecturers reading out chapters from their books, I could manage my time better by going to the library and reading their books – a foolish decision! I spent a lot of my time writing and rewriting that all-important weekly essay, then worrying, drinking endless cups of coffee and chatting with friends.

My tutor, Jonathon Wordsworth, was a handsome man who hid his essential kindness behind a bluff, challenging manner. He actually cared deeply for his students but he was inclined to throw off statements like 'I see from your essay that you've been reading Smith! Well, when I say reading, you've swallowed him whole, like a python with a ruddy great donkey in its stomach!' He seemed to have considerable freedom in the selection of students. He pointed once to the photograph on an application form he'd received from an Australian student. He held the photograph up to the light and asked, 'Shall we have him? He looks like a criminal type to me. I think we should have him!'

He may have exercised this freedom of selection in the case of a late arrival to our group called Barney Walsh. Barney barged his way into the refined world of academia like a cockney chancer intent on stealing the furniture. He was dangerously intelligent and good-looking, but also deeply cynical. As well as our weekly tutorials in English Literature, we had to attend group tutorials in Latin and Anglo-Saxon. Barney must have licked his lips when he saw our Latin tutor, a nervous academic with a squeaky voice and a dry cough, who led us through the complexities of Virgil's Aeneid, book VI. At one point, our tutor chuckled with delight and explained that one of Virgil's descriptions was based on a geographical error. Barney was amused, too. He gave a coarse laugh and exclaimed. 'So old Virgil was buggering up the wrong tree!' The poor tutor tried to share his amusement, but you could see that the effect was unsettling, and it unsettled me too.

But the bad news that we learned soon after our arrival at Exeter College was that Wordsworth wouldn't be teaching our small group of students during our first year. He had delegated the task to a young research student. Here was a man who had once taught Julian Amis and would go on to teach Craig Raine and Philip Pullman. It felt as if we weren't good enough to stimulate his interest. Instead, I had to walk round to a basement flat somewhere in Woodstock Road for a weekly tutorial with a research student who was in bed with his girlfriend when I arrived in his flat. I sat in the armchair in his sitting room, waiting for him to get dressed. His lessons were intelligent and insightful, but I felt immature and out of my depth, exposed to a lifestyle I hadn't yet experienced.

My first term at Oxford should have been easy. I had sold newspapers in Paris! I had hitchhiked to Athens! I had climbed the Parthenon! I had spent a week hosted by Americans on a yacht. Fellow students looked at me and said 'Oh yes,' in a half-interested way, responding more to what they saw than what I said. And what they saw was a young and essentially naive and inexperienced person rabbiting on about his adventures. I had survived up to now chiefly through luck and parental support. I discovered I still had a great deal of growing up left to do.

Acknowledgments

I would like to thank my older sister, Ann, for her encouragement, and for correcting any erroneous statements about our shared past. I would also like to thank my wife, Joey, who is always my sternest critic, and Lauren Etchells, who is a writer herself, and helped me though every aspect of the publishing process.

Also by the Author

Printed in Great Britain
by Amazon

27182751R10046